ISBN 978-1-5285-7002-2
PIBN 10082261

COUNCIL OF NATIONAL DEFENSE
WOMAN'S COMMITTEE

AGENCIES FOR
THE SALE OF COOKED FOODS
WITHOUT PROFIT

A SURVEY OF THEIR DEVELOPMENT
WITH PARTICULAR REFERENCE TO
THEIR SOCIAL AND ECONOMIC EFFECT

Prepared by

IVA LOWTHER PETERS, Ph. D.

Under the direction of

THE FOOD PRODUCTION AND HOME ECONOMICS DEPARTMENT
OF THE WOMAN'S COMMITTEE
COUNCIL OF NATIONAL DEFENSE

WASHINGTON
GOVERNMENT PRINTING OFFICE
1919

WOMAN'S COMMITTEE, COUNCIL OF NATIONAL DEFENSE.

DEPARTMENT OF FOOD PRODUCTION AND HOME ECONOMICS.

Mrs. STANLEY McCORMICK, *chairman.*
Miss HELEN W. ATWATER, *executive chairman.*

ADVISORY COMMITTEE ON SURVEY OF AGENCIES FOR SALE OF COOKED FOODS WITHOUT PROFIT.

Mrs. MARY H. ABEL,
> Writer on Home Economics subjects; Home Economics Director, Maryland Food Administration.

Miss HELEN W. ATWATER,
> Specialist in Home Economics, United States Department of Agriculture.

Dr. SOPHONISBA BRECKINRIDGE,
> Professor, Chicago School of Civics and Philanthropy, Chicago, Ill.

Dr. LUCILE EAVES,
> Director, Research Department, Women's Educational and Industrial Union, Boston, Mass.

Dr. VERNON KELLOGG,
> Professor, Leland Stanford University; United States Food Administration.

Miss MABLE HYDE KITTREDGE,
> Writer and organizer of model housekeeping enterprises, public kitchens, etc., New York City.

Dr. C. F. LANGWORTHY,
> Chief, Office of Home Economics, United States Department of Agriculture.

Dr. RUBY GREEN SMITH,
> Division of Women's Work, Extension Work North and West, United States Department of Agriculture.

2

TABLE OF CONTENTS.

INTRODUCTORY STATEMENT.

The survey here reported was decided upon by the Woman's Committee of the Council of National Defense in the spring of 1918, and the plan for it was developed by an advisory committee of persons known throughout the country for their understanding of the economics of nutrition. At the time when it was undertaken, no one could foresee how food conditions might develop in the United States, and an intelligent policy for national preparedness demanded the collection of reliable information regarding the practical methods and economic results of group or community cooking wherever it had been tried. Although the outcome of the war has now changed the international food situation and there seems less danger of an acute shortage in this country, food conditions are still far from normal. We may yet be called on to share a large proportion of our supplies with less fortunate nations, and prices are still so high that the adequate feeding of many families remains a serious problem. Questions of domestic labor are also becoming more rather than less complicated, both in homes which depend on servants and where the woman who formerly kept house for her own family is now employed outside. Moreover, the general interest in all these questions is much greater than formerly, while reliable information is very scarce. It has, therefore, seemed wise to publish this report, though the original purpose in making it no longer holds.

It is realized fully that the material here presented does not cover the whole subject of the preparation of food outside of the home. Such a complete survey would have involved investigations beyond the functions and means of the Woman's Committee. No effort has been made to include restaurants, even those on a cooperative or community basis, except when they are closely connected with enterprises which sell cooked food to be consumed elsewhere. Commercial canning factories, bakeshops, delicatessen shops, etc., have also been disregarded together with community canning kitchens, cooperative exchanges for home-cooked foods, etc., though the advisory committee is probably unanimous in the belief that if properly controlled as to sanitation and price, some of these offer great promise of relief in this country. The study is limited to noncommercial agencies which strive to remove or lessen the routine preparation of three meals a day in the individual home without weakening the privacy and unity of the family group. The attempt has also been made to include practical information as to organization, management and equipment so that anyone considering the establishment of such an enterprise might profit by previous experience.

In collecting the information here summarized, Mrs. Peters has had access not only to the published documents in the various Government libraries, but also to unpublished material in the files of the United States Food Administration, for whose help and courtesy special acknowledgement should be made.

Similar acknowledgement is due to Mrs. Abel for the use of her unique collection of reports, descriptions, and personal notes concerning the earlier enterprises in this country and abroad. Without this otherwise inaccessible material many sections of the survey would have been impossible.

The committee is also greatly indebted to the Woman's Educational and Industrial Union of Boston and the New York School Lunch Committee of the Association for Improving the Condition of the Poor for permission to print the hitherto unpublished material given in Appendices A and B.

Miss Kittredge and Dr. Kellogg have gone abroad on special missions since the survey was begun and have been unable to pass judgment on the report before its publication. Mrs. Peters also left for overseas service before the manuscript was ready for the press. The final editing (including the formulation of the conclusions) was therefore done by Miss Atwater, who has had immediate direction of the survey from the beginning.

KATHARINE D. McCORMICK,
(Mrs. STANLEY McCORMICK),

Chairman, Department of Food Production and Home Economics, Woman's Committee, Council of National Defense.
JANUARY, 1919.

AGENCIES FOR THE SALE OF COOKED FOODS WITHOUT PROFIT.

A SURVEY OF THEIR DEVELOPMENT WITH PARTICULAR REFERENCE TO THEIR SOCIAL AND ECONOMIC EFFECT.

GENERAL PURPOSE OF THE SURVEY.

As a result of the shortage of food, fuel, and labor occasioned by the great war, nearly all European countries have had recourse to agencies already in existence which had for their purpose the preparation of food in bulk, or have established such agencies on a national scale. The oldest of these agencies were on a charitable or semiphilanthropic basis; some of the largest were cooperative; others were commercial. But all have undergone change to meet the present emergency.

The impression is prevalent that mass feeding of some kind, such as cooperative housekeeping, communal kitchens, or some modified form which will result from experimentation on a large scale, will be retained as a permanent institution after the war. It has been seen by social economists for the past century that the use of such agencies, by taking the kitchen out of the home, would affect not only the cost and quality of the food consumed, but also such questions as those of domestic labor, woman in industry, and would occasion accompanying changes in the economy of the household.

Sporadic attempts to establish agencies for the preparation of food for home consumption have been made in the United States, but for the most part with no lasting success, save in the case of such commercial enterprises as delicatessen shops. The attempts at cooperative housekeeping, of which a record was faithfully kept over a long period by Mrs. Mary Hinman Abel, founder of the New England Kitchen, were chiefly interesting in the light they threw on the psychology of the American people. In a review of the history of the Montclair Cooperative Society, a cooperative venture which was brought to a close by the war, its president, Mr. Emerson P. Harris,[1] called attention to the fact that two fundamental conditions to the success of cooperation almost never exist in the United States—effi-

---

[1] Cooperation, the Hope of the Consumer, by Emerson P. Harris, New York. 1918.

ciency and perseverance on the part of the cooperators and efficient supervision and management. It remains to be seen whether the necessities of the present crisis will lessen our excessive individualism and socialize us to a point where we can live in more closely united communities.

If agencies for communal cooking are introduced into the United States as a result of the necessity for conserving food and fuel, or of reducing cost, it will be of importance to know whether they should be considered as a valuable permanent addition to our national life. The way in which they should be established will depend somewhat upon the answer to this question. Such an answer can be given only after a study of different types of communal feeding. Inasmuch as the development of these types has differed in the various countries in which they have arisen or taken root after introduction from other countries, a brief descriptive and historical survey of these agencies has been undertaken in order to make a fair comparison of the methods used.

This study will first consider the pre-war development of communal agencies for the preparation of food to be consumed in the home. Inasmuch as Great Britain has, as a war measure, established a system of national kitchens, unprecedented in success and development, the second part of the survey will consist of a study of the British national kitchens. The third part will undertake to present the situation in the United States up to November, 1918.

Pre-war experiments in communal feeding lead back in two lines, one, that of cooperative effort, and the other, that of charitable relief.

One form of cooperation which took its rise in the early nineteenth century has had a marvelous development from a small beginning. The direct line of the great English Cooperative Societies, among the largest purveyors of food in the world, leads back to Robert Owen (1771–1858), wealthy factory owner, social reformer, and Utopian dreamer. Owen opened a store in his model factory colony at New Lanark where the people could buy goods of the soundest quality at little more than cost price. In the later elaboration of his theories, he advocated colonies of about 1,200 persons each, who were to be fed from a public kitchen. Owen believed that this method of feeding families would go far toward solving many of the problems of women. His teaching of the necessity of conscious seeking after the welfare of the community, in contrast with the prevailing " laissez-faire " philosophy, his belief in self-supporting communities, and his vision of a new moral and industrial order have left an impress on all classes.

Cooperative societies persisted in England from the time of Owen, with more or less success. Between 1828 and 1840 they reached some 400 or 500. One of these societies had already been formed in Rochdale, in Lancashire, before the Rochdale Equitable Pioneers, in 1844, furnished an administrative method. Appalling need combined with a great idealism in " the hungry forties " brought about the brilliant invention of " dividends on purchases." When the increase in number of cooperative stores on the Rochdale plan brought into existence the Cooperative Wholesale Societies, the venture was made into the field of prepared foods. In 1873 the " C. W. S." started the making of biscuits and sweets. To-day it owns cocoa and chocolate works, preserve, candied peel and pickle works, lard refineries, butter factories, bacon curing, dry-salting and spice-grinding plants, etc. The society has creameries in Ireland, tallow and oil factories in Australia, bacon factories in Denmark and Ireland, 3,386 acres of tea plantations in Ceylon, fruit farms in various parts of England, and great preserving establishments. It owns in the Spanish raisin district a packing house which employs 600 persons in picking, packing and shipping fruit. It owns the largest flour mills in Great Britain. It is the largest single buyer of Canadian wheat, and has recently purchased 10,000 acres of wheat land in Saskatchewan. An authority on the subject makes the statement that the English Co-operative Wholesale is the largest food supply establishment in the world.

All of the European countries had proved fertile ground for the growth of the cooperative movement before the outbreak of the great war, cooperative buying societies frequently developing some form of cooperative-feeding under the pressure of high prices. Impoverished Ireland between 1889 and 1911 formed 934 societies for butter making. Of Denmark, as of Ireland, it has been said that it owes its rebirth since its destructive war with Prussia in 1863–64 to agricultural cooperation. Danish cooperative dairies export butter to the most remote lands. In Sweden, the movement started among the industrialists. Norway reports a cooperative bakery. A Christiania society runs 14 groceries and 3 dairies.

Official Germany tried to discourage the spread of cooperative stores. It was a usual procedure in both Germany and Austria to give members of the stores the choice of retiring from, or expulsion from, any senior military club to which they might belong.[1] But in spite of this opposition, German cooperative societies have a membership of one-half that of England. According to a French report,[2] there were in Germany in 1917, 2,300 societies buying goods at cost and expending 500,000,000 francs. Harris says[3] that the society at Hamburg gained 15,500 members during the year 1916–17. Among the other activities of this society are butcher shops, bakeries, and delicatessen shops. The Government has enlisted the assistance of these societies in the work of establishing public kitchens, which became a necessity in 1916. The question of collective feeding was raised directly in the budget committee of the Landtag of Prussia on November 21 and 23, 1916, and the president of the food office intimated that communal feeding might become obligatory.[4]

Austria was the last of the great European countries to develop cooperation. But in 1867, under the stress of the same crisis which led Dr. von Kühn to inaugurate the Vienna Volksküchen (see p. 17), the societies gained a foothold which they have never lost. The war has seen the formation of the great Victualling Union of War

---

[1] Hans Müller in "The Cooperative Movement Abroad," International Cooperative Bulletin, 1908.

[2] Gilles Normand, La guerre, le commerce français et les consommateurs. Paris, 1917.

[3] Cooperation, the Hope of the Consumer. New York, 1918, p. 230.

[4] Noel Amaudru, Les Cuisines collectives en Allemagne, Bulletin de la Société Scientifique d'Hygiène Alimentaire, Vol. V, No. 6, 1917, p. 359.

Workers, established in 1916, a vast cooperative society of the employees of various industrial enterprises.

The cooperative bakeries of Belgium have had a unique development. Those started at Ghent in the eighties by Edouarde Anseele included among other activities an output of 110,000 loaves of bread a week. Brussels had a society equally large. The dividends from these bakeries were used to form a fund out of which have grown the Vooruit and the Maisons du Peuple. During the great strikes which the workers of Belgium have conducted at various times, free loaves have been distributed from the cooperative bakeries to the unemployed.[1] The Maisons du Peuple, at the time when Germany overran Belgium, were recreational and educational centers with beautiful gardens. Functioning as clubhouses for the people, they provided moving pictures, dances and reading rooms, concerts and dramas.

France was the original home of cooperative production. In spite of the tragedy of the Commune, cooperative workshops had persisted, and in 1910 were reported as doing an annual business of $10,000,000. The statistical tables prepared by M. Charles Gide,[2] show that the French tendency in cooperative ventures, as contrasted with those in Anglo-Saxon countries, has been toward decentralization. One-third of the French societies are bakeries, and most of the stores sell only groceries. Since the beginning of the war the cooperatives of Paris, at the request of the Government, have taken over the frozen-meat trade. They have also reestablished the shops of the French-Swiss society, "Maggi," where milk, butter, and eggs were sold, and have been keeping down the price of milk.

Their development is discussed in a report of a special mission sent to France by the British ministry of food:[3]

In numbers of French towns where there were no cooperative societies the inhabitants, sometimes with the help of the municipality, have formed leagues to fight against exploitation by local dealers. Cooperative bakeries are being formed at the front. But communal preparation of food has not developed in France along the lines now familiar in England, Germany, Austria, and Italy.

Now, even more than in peace time, the cooking of food is regarded in France as a fine art. The sustenance afforded by good food well cooked is a fundamental fact of the war to which French men and women are keenly alive. The ministry's representatives found this to be the case particularly in the canteens used by industrial workers, which are very efficiently managed. The same establishment had attached to it a crèche, and here mothers, while they worked, were able to leave their babies, whom they could visit at stated

[1] "A Baker and What He Baked," by Albert Sonnichsen. The Outlook, Dec. 27, 1913.
[2] Les Sociétés Cooperatives de Consummation, p. 38.
[3] National Food Journal, Nov. 14, 1917, p. 78.

hours. The men and women have their meals together and share their rest rooms. A popular feature in some canteens is a "heating-up" room, where wives who bring their husbands' meals can warm the food on hot plates, after the American style, and then stay and partake of the meal in company with their husbands in the communal dining room. The work performed by the canteens in providing good fare amid comfortable surroundings is of particular merit by reason of the fact that the advances in the price of foodstuffs far outstrip the increases in wages.

In spite, however, of this strong conservatism with reference to any change in the habits of the French family, recent reports are significant of approaching change along lines for which our study of French cooperative movements has prepared us. In a special cable appearing in the New York Times on September 18, 1918, the writer says:

The French belief in collectivism as a political economic faith is probably stronger to-day than ever, in view of the rampant profiteering by almost every class of retail trader since the war began.

A cable to the same newspaper dated September 11, 1918, states that Finance Minister Klotz has announced that:

The French Government would take vigorously in hand the question of stopping the artificial rise in the prices of all necessaries in the way of foodstuffs, which in the last few weeks has assumed little short of monstrous proportions. Taking the view that the only effective remedy will be to suppress the abusive profits of intermediaries, the Government has appointed an interministerial committee to study the best means of placing at the disposal of the population of the country, in best condition as to price and quality, necessaries in the way of foodstuffs, and more particularly measures which may be taken in this direction for the benefit of those engaged in public services, by the creation of cooperative agencies, canteens, and organizations for meals in common.

Italy has been a fruitful field for all forms of cooperative societies. The unique cooperative labor group, the "Societa di Lavoro," has been her contribution to the movement. The large cooperative union in Milan had sales in 1916 of almost 24,000,000 lire as against 15,000,000 in 1915. The foundation of the war restaurants of Mantua, Florence, Milan, Rome, Bologna, Turin, and other Italian cities was often the restaurants that had existed in the cooperative societies' stores.

When we turn to the annals of cooperative movements in America to find a possible background for the development of communal feeding, we find that this country has been the grave of such ventures, from such great adventures as the colony of Owen at New Harmony, Ind., and the romantic Brook Farm experiment, down to the humblest and most practical attempt at cooperative housekeeping. There are scattered across the continent to-day some hundreds of isolated cooperative stores. But the isolation which has fostered the over-individuation of Americans has prevented the growth of groups with the true spirit of cooperation, the element which has hitherto been lacking. Whether the present crisis will force into our hands a tool as perfected as is the Rochdale plan of cooperation, remains to be seen. It is worth remembering, however, that in none of the countries where such cooperative societies have proved generally successful have they had commercial competitors organized as are the so-called " chain stores " and large mail-order houses of the United States.

We have thus far dealt with a medium for production and distribution of food which was worked by the private initiative of thrifty and farsighted members of society, who needed no instruction from members of another social class in the principles of " self-help." But in every social group are to be found the careless, the thriftless, and improvident, as well as those who through misfortune must be helped by others. In old and densely populated communities agencies have been developed to care for these groups as well as to provide for the feeding of large numbers in times of famine, war, and epidemics. Inseparably connected with the problems of mass feeding raised by such classes and conditions is the name of Benjamin Thompson, Count Rumford, British-American scientist, administrator, and philanthropist.

At the close of the eighteenth century, a period when there was in existence only the scanty body of facts that made up the beginning of chemistry, physiology, and physics, Count Rumford brought to the choice and preparation of food on a large scale the insight and methods of the scientist. During the 11 years spent by him in Bavaria on the invitation of Prince Maximilian, he improved the food of the Bavarian Army without materially increasing its cost. In an effort to solve the food problem of the poor, he caused no fewer than 2,600 beggars of Munich to be arrested by military patrols and transferred to an industrial establishment called the House of Industry. Here they were fed, not with the ordinary food of the country, but with a nutritious soup with dried peas and barley as the basis. Already interested in the problem of heat, he studied the effect of water at different temperatures on the ingredients of his new food. Stoves were constructed for economy in the use of fuel. As a result of his inventions, it was found that 1,000 portions of soup in summer and 1,200 in winter could be cooked and served with bread at a cost of one-third of a farthing a portion. Kitchens of this same type were established in Dublin and Ireland. The soup served in them is still the main food of inmates of Houses of Industry on the Continent. No real advance on the foundation laid by Count Rumford was made in later efforts to improve the food of the poor until our own time.

It has been said of Count Rumford that, being a scientific man, he put nutrition too far above attractiveness; and that it may have been from his efforts that the tradition arose that " cheap food is nasty." It is probable, however, that the surroundings and associations under which the food was served had much to do with the tradition. However this may be, there is no doubt that the prejudices of many kinds which cluster about communal feeding have been serious impediments to the success of these ventures. Perhaps when the psychology of nutrition is better understood, we shall be able to cope with these hindrances with greater intelligence. But in spite of tradition, it is of interest to note that when the exigencies of war compelled Germany to try the experiment of cost-price public kitchens and aided workpeople's kitchens, Munich and Bavaria led the way. By November, 1916, Munich was giving a course of instruction in the management of these kitchens.

There have been several noteworthy experiments in cheap catering in the various European countries since the middle of the nineteenth century. They have combined the discoveries of Count Rumford and his successors with the various developments of the cooperative movement, and have adapted them to meet the conditions of the countries and classes with whom they were dealing. Some of the most noteworthy will be briefly described.

The first " people's kitchen " opened in Germany with the avowed purpose of complete freedom from any eleemosynary taint, while at the same time it was to be kept free from the clutches of the profiteer, was organized by the Hülfs-Verein of Leipzig in 1849. It was a part of the effort of public spirited persons of different professions to cope with the misery which threatened the professional as well as the working classes as the result of business depression. The kitchen was placed under careful direction and oversight, and all labor was paid. Staples were purchased in quantity and sold at cost to the members of the Verein. The success of this venture was proved by the fact that during its first year no less than 122,000 sales were made, and in the 22 years following there was a yearly average of 177,562 sales. Another kitchen of the same character was opened in 1871 in another part of Leipzig, whose sales annually exceeded 400,000. Vienna, Zurich, Hanover, Berlin, Halle, Monaco, Gratz, London, Eilenberg, and Bradford later opened kitchens on the model of the original at Leipzig.

During the mid-century period of economic distress which affected all Europe, a kitchen was opened in Geneva under different auspices. A group of 60 workingmen, with a social capital of only 60 francs, secured rent-free quarters from the municipality in which they established a common table and served wholesome, nutritious food at minimum cost. This Swiss organization continued for several years with great usefulness to its members, but finally passed out of existence. An observer and well-wisher thought the failure of such a worthy venture was the result of the lack of a solid basis of direction and oversight. But the experiment lasted long enough for many observers to see the advantage of the preparation of food in quantity, to be sold to members at cost. A member of the faculty of the university at Grenoble, France, doubtless familiar with the Geneva experiment, established in 1850 a similar association with 800 members. The Grenoble city council, as at Geneva, stood back of the experiment, but was only to aid in case of a deficit. The venture seems to have proven successful, as no such contingency arose.

The organizations at Leipzig, Geneva, and Grenoble, as well as the earlier English experiments, were chiefly concerned with the economies of the food problem. In June, 1860, Mr. Thomas Corbett, of Glasgow, in a study of "The Kitchen of the Poor," lamented that the food question, much studied from the standpoint of price and of the prevention of pauperism, could not be approached from the standpoint of some of the other equally acute problems of the self-respecting working classes. He instanced the possibility of a connection between the effect of badly-prepared, unsatisfying food and the increase of intemperance. As a result of this careful study, the first "economic kitchen" was established in Glasgow. The purpose of this kitchen was to give the self-respecting worker attractive food at a reasonable price. Everything possible was done to prevent the venture being looked upon as a philanthrophy or charity. It was started by fixing the price of every portion at a penny, to continue if this proved a "paying proposition." The first kitchen was opened in September, 1860. Its success was so great that another was almost immediately opened. As a result of the success of the Glasgow kitchens, Manchester, Liverpool, Birmingham, and other industrial cities made ventures along the same line.

The founder of the Italian "Cucini popolari" in the exact sense of the term was Signor Cav. Bigotti, of Modena. In the winter of 1879–80, one of great distress among the poor, Signor Bigotti with the assistance of a committee of fellow citizens opened a kitchen. Although its original purpose was to aid the very needy, the work was extended to include the better working classes. It is a significant fact that when this organization is compared with the "penny kitchens" of Glasgow, we find that the founders of the Italian enterprise do not have to guard against the "touchiness" in the workmen as do all interested in English and Scotch ventures. The Italian founders advocate private control as "introducing a moral element not possible with an impersonal organization," and say that "personal cooperation between the giver and receiver gives the best results." While this is accepted in principle by all the followers of Saint-Simon as a means for the prevention of class conflict, in praetice it has often been found, at least among Anglo-Saxons, that the relation of giver and receiver is hard to maintain without friction.[1]

The peoples' kitchens of Vienna are said to be the most important of their kind in Europe, not excepting the Volksküchen of Berlin, which are a few years older. In each case the origin can be traced to the initiative of a single person, Dr. Joseph von Kühn in Vienna and Frau Lina Morgenstern in Berlin.

The plan of organization of the Volksküchen of Austria and Germany is much the same. There is a central committee made up of public-spirited men and women serving without pay. This committee manages all the finances, and is a court of last appeal. Each kitchen has its own committee, the chairman being a member of the central committee. The local committee manages the business of its kitchen, keeps the books, etc., and reports at stated intervals to the central committee. In each case the kitchens are capitalized by contributions from philanthropic persons, and it is expected that all the work of the committee shall be unrecompensed. The original contribution to the Berlin kitchen, 4,359 thalers (about $3,000), had grown by profits and gifts to 95,000 marks in 1890. No interest is paid on this fund, nor on several other funds used to pension employees, etc. All superintendence is unpaid. Aside from these forms of indirect assistance, the sale of the food is expected to support the kitchens. The purchase or rent of a building, the laying in of stock, and the wages of the paid help, are the necessary expenses. Frau Morgenstern in one of her reports says that ladies in Berlin were eager to serve as waitresses, for the Volksküchen were the first outside activity permitted to women of the better classes in many communities of the Teutonic countries. The plans for opening a kitchen are carefully worked out to the last detail, and printed, so that, to quote Frau Morgenstern, "the failure of a kitchen means either bad management or the lack of need of the kitchen in that locality." Even the recipes for a kitchen such as the one in Berlin may be obtained for a few pfennigs. But with all the minute Teutonic care with which details have been worked out (directions even being given as to provision for the cook's children, if she has any), these kitchens do not run themselves.

Their founder, looking back over 25 years of service, comments:

In order to be successful, they demand devotion, a great deal of personal supervision, and initiative on the part of the organizers. They require practical understanding, good business management, with a knowledge of proper location. And above all, they demand tact, insight, and a love of humanity.

---

[1] Much of the information given above concerning the early "peoples' kitchens" was obtained from a study made by Prof. L. Pagliani, and presented in 1883 at the Conferenza pubblica popolari della sede Piemontese della societa Italiana d'igiene.

Special interest attaches to the work in Vienna owing to the fact that it was from the first, self-supporting. It started on humble lines. The great success it achieved was due to skillful organization, careful management, and infinite taking of pains.

After the Austro-Prussian war, when many members of the working class starved to death in Austria, Dr. von Kühn gave up his post as a state official to study measures to lessen the evil. He began by a study of the provision trade. As a result of this study, he became impressed, as had the great German economist Schulze-Delitsch in 1848, with the exorbitant profits of those who sell to the poor. Dr. von Kühn interested four friends in his plan, and with them organized an executive committee. One was secretary, another treasurer, while Dr. von Kühn became chairman. Each subscribed 1,000 kronen. With this sum (about $1,000) they started a Volksküche in a section of Vienna where poverty was rife. Its success was so great that in 1872, Dr. von Kühn gave up all other work and devoted all his time and energy up to his death in 1913 to controlling and directing the work of the Volksküchen. He bought the provisions, engaged the servants, and decided what should be cooked and how. He was always in the kitchens when dinner was being served, tasting every dish before it was served, and watching those who ate the dishes to see which they liked best. When the Volksküchen began to sell food for home consumption, they became more popular than ever.

The Vienna Volksküchen, one of which was in operation in every district of the city in 1914, are worked on business principles. Patrons go as to an ordinary store or restaurant and pay for what they buy what it costs. As the question of what constitutes a " cost price " is still a mooted one in all these ventures, it is of interest to know what was included in this successful kitchen. The original cost of the ingredients, the cost of preparation and cooking, a carefully calculated proportion of the cost of lighting, heating, and the general upkeep of the kitchens, were considered. Whenever it was found that there was a profit, the price of the food sold was reduced. Another great difference from the ordinary commercial venture is that no interest was paid on the original investment made by Dr. von Kühn and his friends. The working expenses were further lowered by the fact that much was done by the " honorary officials," as in the peoples' kitchens in Germany, where the work has been a part of the accepted charity work of every society woman, much as Red Cross work is in war time. Soon after the opening of the first kitchen, Dr. von Kühn persuaded a friend to become lady superintendent. It was her business to watch over the matron, the cook, and other servants, and to play hostess to all comers. Committees of ladies were formed to act as waitresses in the kitchens. For years all the waiting in the kitchens was done by ladies.

The Vienna kitchens were at first open only from 11.30 a. m. to 2 p. m. A 3-penny dinner was served, which consisted of a slice of beef, mutton, pork, or veal, with a large dish of vegetables. He who had only a penny could have soup, vegetables, or a dish of savory rice with bread. A woman familiar with the restaurants of England states that in 1914 a better dinner could be bought in Vienna for a fraction over 5d. than in any English restaurant for 10d., with the exception of the Alexandra Trust Dining Rooms. (See below.)

In the 15 kitchens of Vienna in 1914 there were 2,756 seats, and each seat could be filled eight times during the dinner hours. Thus 22,048 men and women could have their dinners there, in addition to the thousands who bought dinners they took home. In the case of every successful kitchen of this type studied by the writer, it has been found necessary to give the two kinds of service. The Berlin kitchens started with the avowed intention of serving no meals on the premises. But from the first there were deserving patrons who pled to be permitted to eat in the chimney corner, so that more or less reluctantly this service was provided. One reason for this is the difficulty in keeping the food hot. Patrons are usually expected to provide their own receivers, which makes another difficulty for those who stop on the way to and from their working places.

Prior to 1914 the enterprises in England most closely resembling the German and Austrian Volksküchen were the Alexandra Trust Dining Rooms in London. These were directly inspired by the Viennese Volksküchen. The fare is more varied than in many people's kitchens and less suggestive of Rumford's soup kitchens. On one dinner menu were found the following items: Clear soup, vegetable soup, beef venison with macaroni, pork cutlets with salad, spinach, peas, fruit pudding, and ginger pudding. But the initial expenses were much heavier than those of their Austrian or German prototypes. It was estimated in 1914 that to start such a kitchen in England would require a capital of from $2,000 to $2,500.

The peoples' kitchens have been utilized as a partial solution of the problem of feeding school children, a duty which is coming to the fore in every country. In 1914 the Vienna kitchens provided dinners for 5,420 school children at a charge just under a penny for soup, or milk pudding, or vegetables, served with a large roll. The Alexandra Trust Dining Rooms send out 45,000 meals for school children on school days in addition to the 4,000 meals served to other clients from day to day. A child is charged less than half the price charged an adult. In spite of this the plan has for years been self-supporting. It is of interest to Americans to note in this connection that a venture of this type, the New England Kitchen of Boston, was launched in 1890 by two women who were close students of the European kitchens, Mrs. Mary Hinman Abel and Mrs. Ellen H. Richards. The original New England Kitchen was put on its feet financially in two years chiefly by its proximity to an educational institution, to which for the first three years of its existence the kitchen served 300 lunches daily at a cost of 15 cents per person. It is said that the school luncheons served by the New England Kitchen were "the first American effort to deal in a scientific way with the nourishment of school children."[1]

The Peoples' Kitchens Associations are the great emergency caterers for Austria and Germany. The Vienna Association has an engagement with the State under which it it responsible for the feeding of 10,000 persons at 24 hours' notice. The equipment of an emergeney kitchen is kept ready packed in a large van, the food needed is sent direct from the central kitchen in air-tight cans in which food will retain its heat for 24 hours. Both the Red Cross and the war office draw on the kitchens. The German Volksküchen, with headquarters in Berlin, are similarly organized. Almost immediately after their founding in 1866, they were called upon to test their organization through the great outbreak of cholera. Then came the Franco-Prussian War, in which their service was so great as to establish them firmly as an institution. .

From the scanty information to be gathered as to the development of the Volksküchen in Germany and Austria under the stress of the great war, it would seem that they show greater differences than in their earlier evolution. The taint of the philanthropic "soup kitchen" seems to have affected the kitchens of Germany more than those of Austria. The German kitchens had a more direct descent from the Rumford kitchens, and seem never to have catered to individual taste by a varied menu as did the kitchens founded by Dr. von Kühn. Consultation of the booklet of directions for the opening of a kitchen on the Berlin model shows a paucity of recipes and of cooking utensils.

The cooperative ventures, on the other hand, seem to have gained marvelously from the war, as shown by statistics. The new ventures in Germany in cost-price kitchens and aided workpeoples' kitchens are aided by the State and municipalities. In many cases town councils provide capital, equipment, and even grants. The Bürger-Zeitung of Bremen made the statement in June, 1916, that the kitchens of Hamburg were receiving 401,000 marks a month from the war fund. But either from their ancient reputation, or from other causes, it is reported that the workers are not attracted by the kitchens, and go only as a last resort. It is said that in Hamburg the

---

[1] The Food of Working Women in Boston, Women's Educational and Industrial Union, Boston, 1917.

manageress is assisted in maintaining order by trades-union representatives, which gives some insight into the complication involved in the maintenance of the system. In all the German war kitchens, with very few exceptions, the food may be eaten on the premises or taken home. The most popular ones seem to be those established by the large munition works for their own employees. which are run in much the same way as those in France (see p. 12). In many cases the families of the workers are permitted to eat at these kitchens. But all German reports agree that municipal feeding has no future in Germany.[1]

The Austrian tradition concerning "soup kitchens" seems to have been less binding, or their inauguration as a war measure was under happier auspices. In May, 1917, a central office for the supply of foodstuffs was created, and an association of war kitchens was formed to deal with the central office. The group system, similar to the older experiments at Geneva and Grenoble, has been utilized. Middle-class kitchens have been kept distinct from those run on philanthropic lines; there have been public kitchens patronized by groups of people—not only employees in the same business, but professionals, such as university teachers and actors. The older form of the Volksküchen persists, but is kept strictly apart in administration from the middle-class kitchens. Nevertheless this group system is said to have aroused bitter comment. Certain sets or cliques have been favored, and if one does not "belong to" something for public feeding, or for supply of foodstuffs at home, one is out in the cold and stands in queues. But in spite of these administrative evils, it is clearly to be seen that the group system has many advantages. It does not entail so much of "psychic shock" in the change of food habits, which is apt to have serious effects with older persons. More than this, there are group likes and dislikes in food, as well as racial differences, and it is easier for a kitchen to cater to the tastes of one class only.

The experiments at communal feeding, mass feeding, or of providing food in bulk, which we have considered so far, have all been concerned with the complete elimination of profit. As we have seen, it is difficult in all undertakings which aim to be other than charities, to define what shall be legitimately included in "cost price." Many of these ventures, including the Volksküchen, eliminate certain legitimate costs, such as return on capital invested, so that they are technically charities, although perhaps no more so than our great educational institutions. Frau Morgenstern acutely observes in the "History of the Volksküchen" that these institutions give

[1] Communal Kitchens in European Countries, by Anice L. Whitney, Monthly Review of the Bureau of Labor Statistics, June, 1918; see also article on Administrative Methods in Other Countries, National Food Journal, vol. 1, No. 15, Apr. 10, 1918, pp. 393, 394.

back their interest to the state in the prevention of epidemics arising from malnutrition. But there have been ventures in the preparation of wholesome food at a reduced price which have paid their way in the commerical sense. Among these are the Christiania Steam Kitchen, started in 1857, and to-day as thriving as some of the great English cooperative stores, and the Kvindernes Kökken of Copenhagen, a shop-girls' restaurant. These two undertakings are neither cooperative nor philanthropic, but are commercial agencies, though of an unusual type.[1]

The Christiania Steam Kitchen was started in 1857 by a group of business men—merchants, an official, a lawyer, and the chief of police—who were anxious to help the luckless, but wise enough to know that they could help by taking thought, and not by lavishing money. Believing that they could best help by providing wholesome food at the lowest price at which it could be sold and keep the place of sale absolutely self-supporting, they started a stock company with a working capital of 3,483 pounds, and opened the steam kitchen. They enacted that not more than 6 per cent interest should be paid on the capital invested. They built the kitchen in the middle of the town, and installed an expert cook. The purchasing was done by the members of the company.

Although the place proved popular, it ran with a deficit until 1866, when an attempt was made to attract middle-class custom by opening a department in which uncooked food was sold. This proved such a success that the price of cooked provisions could be reduced without incurring a loss. The kitchen was twice enlarged, and has now been rebuilt. It is a huge place, with a paid general manager, a paid manager for each department, and other paid officials, all of whom are under the direction of a board of directors chosen by the shareholders. In 1914 working expenses were only 8.7 per cent of the turnover. Fifteen hundred men and women ate dinner there every day; 100 more bought in the cooked food department dinners to be eaten at home.

The Kvindernes Kökken of Copenhagen, a shopgirls' restaurant which serves meals daily to from 1,200 to 1,800 women beside those who buy their food and take it home, is also a business undertaking, not a charity. It was planned entirely, and in 1914 was still directed, by two lower middle class women who had thoughtfully watched the failure of a philanthropic venture started with the same purpose. They took over the plant as a going concern, and paid for its fittings by installments. They employed as cooks highly trained experts in their craft. Their assistants are appren-

---

[1] Article by Edith Sellers in The 19th Century and After, 76, No. 453 (November, 1914); also Inexpensive Restaurants, by Helen W. Atwater, Journal of Home Economics, vol. VIII, No. 6 (June, 1916).

tices who go to the Kökken as to a technical school, receiving no
wages. The waitresses are daughters of pastors, teachers, and officials. The rooms are carefully and tastefully furnished. In each
dressing room there is an official, chosen for kindliness. In such
ways is the tone of the establishment maintained.

The Kökken opens at 9 a. m. The place is crowded between 11
and 1, and again between 5 and 6. No man is admitted except as
the guest of a woman. There is a choice between a la carte service and a regular dinner, which consists of two courses, good in
quality and unlimited in quantity. In 1914 such a dinner as veal
with new potatoes and an excellent sauce, bread, apricots, and milk
cost 14 cents. For 4 cents more soup was added, and a cup of
coffee for $2\frac{3}{4}$ cents.

Both of these ventures in low-priced catering have probably been
affected by the war, which has very seriously altered the cost of
living in the Scandinavian countries.

The first public kitchens in Denmark, as might be expected, were
not charitable in any sense of the word. Both Denmark and Sweden
are said to prefer the delivery of cooked food at home to service in
restaurants.

Such a survey as has been undertaken in these pages makes it
evident that the idea of mass feeding and of the preparation of
wholesome food for consumption in the home at a reduced price
was not new in Europe in 1914. The machinery of such ventures
had been worked out, and a study of cheap and nutritious foods
had been made. Social workers had repeatedly urged their adoption
as a solution of other problems than those purely economic. The
accelerated absorption of women into the war industries merely
intensified a condition to which economists and sociologists had
been calling attention for half a century, a condition which was
already apparent to thinkers at the beginning of the nineteenth
century, but whose amelioration was to wait for slower processes
of adjustment than those advocated by Fourier and Owen.

Opposition to the more ambitious schemes for the preparation of
food in bulk has usually included some statement that a definite
movement of this nature would accelerate the decay of family life.
This is a serious charge, if true. Sociological research has made
it clear that the component group we call the family is " the cradle
of our social ideals and the natural environment for the child, and
that a normal family life is at the basis of social life in general."
But the development of industrial life makes it increasingly evident that it is to the need for woman in the life outside the home
that we must look for the causation of the decay of family industry, and that the weighing of the economic value of woman's
work will finally be a deciding factor in the changes in family

life to meet the new order. If a radical change in the accepted way of insuring wholesome food to persons of scanty or moderate means should emerge from the present crisis, a change which would touch the most serious problems of poverty—the feeding of children, the nutrition of the mother, the care of the aged and orphans—it might carry with it a solution of other problems involving the happiness and unity of families. It may be that wife desertion, abandonment of children, crimes against property, even murder, are often traceable to scanty and poor food, a contributor to the misery of the poor. If the people's kitchens could be made to render more abundant and wholesome the nutrition of poor families, and at the same time lighten the load resting on the shoulders of the wife and mother, there is no doubt we should increase the mutual respect and affection of their members. And if it were not for the blow to the pride of the great middle class, as much might be said of it. It is a recognized fact among students of nutrition that it is not always lack of money which prevents the serving of wholesome food. Miss Sellers, an Englishwoman, ventures the statement that the man of the lower middle class in England is perhaps the poorest nourished, and Arnold Bennett has made plain the fallacy upon which English and Americans alike have traded, that housewives are "born" and need not be trained. It may be the beginning of a better day for others than the very poor when some agency other than an ignorant woman with no taste for cooking is left to cope with what is coming to be seen as a science—the choice and preparation of a balanced diet. Dr. Vernon Kellogg calls attention to the fact that one of the very interesting developments of the war has been the establishment of communal kitchens for the middle class which pay their own expenses and are recognized as of the greatest convenience to their patrons.

But no rationalizing forces or philanthropic influences lie back of the present spread of communal kitchens in Europe. They are the outhgrowth of sheer necessity. All that philanthrophy or the social sciences can be said to have done was to prepare the minds of the people for them and to have worked out methods, such as the Volksküchen and the cooperating stores. The introduction of rationing, the difficulty of getting food and the annoying waiting in queues, and, to a less extent, the lack of fuel, were primary causes. Their success has depended upon the fact that one could get more value for the food card at the kitchen than one could get at home. Whenever the rations are generous, it is said that the attendance at the German kitchens falls off, in spite of facilities for the delivery of cooked meals. A picture of the situation in Austria is given in an article entitled "How the Viennese Live," written by Leonhard Adelt from

Vienna to the Berliner Tageblatt, and printed in the issue of July 9, 1918:

The supplying of Austria rests with state controlled economic groups which regulate consumption and sales, and the Food Centrals, which, like the War Grain Exchanges establishment and the Fodder Central or like the Oezeg (Austrian Central Buying Association), and the Geos (vegetable and food supply establishment), are under the control of the imperial and royal office for the nation's food. * * *

As in all the warring countries the economic and social clashes have become sharper in Austria. The piling up of wealth on the part of a small group is accompanied by the rapid loss of the middle classes and the helplessness of the lowest class as a result of the decreased purchasing power of money. For the benefit of the poorest class the Government some time ago established a credit for needy of more than $60,000,000. Meals and cheap war kitchens for the middle class and the workers complete the State's aid.[1]

---

[1] Selections from a translation of the article printed in the New York Times, Sunday, Sept. 1, 1918.

A chronological study of the preparation of the conservative British middle class for the idea of communal cooking will be enlightening to the American reader. Credit for the success of the plan rests with the food controller, Lord Rhondda, "one of the few great men the war discovered."

Under Lord Rhondda's direction, a food economy campaign was inaugurated. Sir Arthur Yapp, national secretary of the Y. M. C. A., was appointed director of food economy in the ministry of food in September, 1917. It was announced that the campaign was to be directed not only to the serious situation confronting the nation at the moment, but to the situation after the war. The campaign was to utilize all existing machinery, churches and chapels, universities and schools, corporations, members of Parliament, women's societies, etc. In the same month the ministry of food began the publication of the National Food Journal, whose avowed purpose was "informational and educational." In the first issue, September 12, 1917, the vital necessity of food economy was shown to be not only temporary. Statistics were quoted as to the decrease in the world's meat producing animals. Economies could be effected by people eating less, by the elimination of waste, and by the use of all foodstuffs to the greatest nutritive advantage. The number contained this paragraph relative to the central kitchen movement, already under way:

Attention has been given to the reduction of food consumption by teaching improved kitchen economy, as the waste due to ill-chosen and ill-prepared food among the wage-earning section of the population has always been considerable. The most hopeful line of approach has been found to consist in the establishment of central or communal kitchens where cooked food is served and demonstrations are given showing how food can be prepared with the maximum of nutrition and the minimum of waste.

In the issue of the Journal for September 26, it was again pointed out that the danger of the food situation lay not so much in the submarine peril as in the world shortage of cereals, meats, and fats; and the high prices were ascribed to the fact that England was paying for her important imported food stuffs more than double what she paid before the war. The Daily Telegraph was quoted:

The fundamental fact of the food situation is that the supplies of most commodities, not only in this country, but all the world over, fall below the usual production. This state of things would not be altered if peace were declared to-morrow, and will certainly exist for some time after the war has come to an end.

To meet the situation, the unnecessary middle-man must be eliminated. Lord Rhondda recommended—always a strong point with him—the utilization of existing agencies under license and control, and under the supervision of local food controllers appointed by the local authorities.

Before the inauguration of the food economy campaign the ministry of food had been experimenting with central kitchens, later defined as " kitchens established to buy raw foodstuffs and to sell cooked foods with a view to conserving the foodstuffs of the country, especially its cereals, that is to say, its wheat and wheat substitutes." A model kitchen was opened on May 31, 1917, by the ministry in Westminster Bridge Road, London. Even before this date, local committees had been experimenting so widely that an Englishwoman, writing on the subject in June, prophesied that " nine out of ten will fail. The tenth may scramble through, more by good luck than good management." This critic believed in the principle of the kitchens, but not in the method of organization and control at first in vogue, when the kitchens were still " muddling through." She writes: " They can reopen later and be conducted under proper control with the valuable assistance of catering and domestic science departments, and with trained workers instead of amateurs."

But not all the first trial kitchens were failures. · Hammersmith, whose mayor was the first to subsidize the equipment of a public kitchen out of the rates, had a central kitchen in operation from March, 1917, and in February, 1918, reported 9 depots. Two kitchens opened in May in West Ham were so successful that three others were added with satisfactory results. Up to December, 1917, these five kitchens served nearly 50,000 meals to all classes of people, at an average of 5d. each. At these kitchens, the prices vary from a penny to six pence per portion. In addition to providing food to be taken away by the people for consumption at home, the original intention of all the kitchens, there was such a demand for dining rooms in connection with the kitchen that two were built, one for each sex.

On the basis of the experience of the ministry of food with experimental kitchens and kitchens opened by local authorities, a memorandum was prepared in the autumn of 1917, defining the objects for which it was intended that central kitchens should be established, and setting out methods of establishment and management.[1]

It is recommended as a general rule that central kitchens be established only for the prepartion and supply of cooked food to be consumed off the premises; but it would sometimes be advisable, where there is a large and populous area to be served, to arrange in addition for a number of distributing depots. Kitchens were to be self-supporting as far as possible. They should be free from the element of charity and so conducted that any person might use them with self-respect.

By the close of 1917 it was apparent that assistance in the initial cost of equipment was necessary. In a speech delivered at the opening of the communal kitchen in North Woolwich Road, Silvertown, West Ham, Lord Rhondda said that "orders had been issued empowering local authorities to establish and control kitchens, and grants would be made to the authorities which advanced the money." When the Marylebone Borough council decided in December, 1917, to establish and equip a central municipal kitchen for cooking and supplying food for the inhabitants of the borough, it was with the understanding that the Government would contribute 25 per cent of the cost, and advance by way of loan for the establishment of the kitchen another 25 per cent, free of interest.[1]

All was not clear sailing for the ministry of food in its dealing with local boards. Some were too ambitious. Under date of November 27, 1917, in the London Times there appeared the following:

The St. Pancras food control committee has expressed the opinion to the ministry that if premises such as large restaurants, hotels, clubs, and public institutions were utilized for the cooking of meals, and if a suitable transport scheme were arranged to convey the cooked food to municipal distributing centers, public feeding on a large scale could be quickly organized without having to wait for new plant and adaptation of buildings.

This attempt to start on the grand scale touched on what was to be one of the most puzzling questions, how to deal with local caterers. It took all the patience and tact of both Lord Rhondda and his able assistant and successor, Mr. Clynes, to deal with this problem. In actual practice, it is probably true that much friction and waste could have been avoided if, in the framing of schemes, local committees had taken account of the catering facilities in the area, had consulted with the proprietors, and agreed upon a plan whereby all the establishments in the neighborhood could be brought together into one comprehensive system. That some attempts to placate local dealers were made is evident. The Marylebone Borough council, in the announcement of its plan for a kitchen, emphasized the statement that "there will not be any attempt to undersell local traders." The founder of a chain of restaurants well known in London complained bitterly in the columns of the press that the national kitchens were "cruelly unjust to the existing caterer, who is responsible for leaseholds and has the whole of his capital invested in his business."

---

[1] London Times, Dec. 28, 1917, p. 3.

"The promoters of the national kitchens," he said, "have a preference in regard to marketing, and enjoy a priority in respect of staff,
utensils, stoves, boilers, and other matters connected with output."
As early as January, 1918, he had suggested to the ministry of food
that they should take over the working-class restaurants. In his
reply, Mr. Clynes has said, as he had said repeatedly in response to
parliamentary inquiries on this subject: "Our object is to supple-
ment the efforts of others, and to meet a very pressing war-time
demand."[1]

In view of this a statement was later made in the press that the
food controller had refused to establish national kitchens in communities where the borough is amply catered for with regard to the
supply of cooked food at reasonable prices. The ministry was ready
to consider a scheme whereby caterers could be supplied with raw
materials and appliances on a reasonable basis. But if this were
done they must limit their prices and their profits in the interests of
the public.[2]

The experiments with central kitchens in 1917 had raised other
objections. In spite of Lord Rhondda's statements as to the vital
necessity of the kitchens, it was much discussed whether there was
a real need for them. Both the food controller and the director of
food economy repeatedly urged upon local committees the importance of being prepared with the necessary arrangements for feeding
masses of the people, should there be any serious breakdown of food
supplies. But in their reports on the subject some local committees
insisted that there was no poverty apparent in their boroughs; that
the food shortage was not sufficiently acute to make the kitchens an
urgent and immediate necessity; and that owing to the high rate of
wages the high prices of commodities were not being felt as they
would be in normal times.

In spite of objectors, the success of the experimental kitchens and
the food economy campaign had led by January, 1917, to the establishment of communal kitchens at more than 60 centers, including
Leeds, Manchester, Sheffield, Gloucester, Reading, Oxford, Ipswich,
Chester, Dorking, Bailey, Halifax, Croyden, Broadstairs, Bourne-
mouth, Cheltenham, Folkestone, Middlesbrough, Sunderland, Tor-
quay, Welshpool, Watford, West Hartlepool, and in many of the
London boroughs. But the need was too pressing to wait for local
authorities to take the initiative. The propaganda for voluntary
economy was discontinued. In January, 1918, Alderman C. F.
Spencer, of Halifax, a successful business man, was asked by Lord
Rhondda to come to the ministry of food and take up at once the

task of developing the branch of the department which dealt with communal kitchens. On February 1 Mr. Spencer gave particulars of his schemes for setting up kitchens in places outside of London, including the following: [1]

Transport of food.—Electric kitchens, on the trains, in which the food would be kept hot; and also to use gas-bag motors and traveling kitchens. His scheme will even provide for keeping warm small quantities of food bought by individuals * * *. The good will of the people was needed when it came to a change in the national habits of feeding the community.

The advantage and utility of national kitchens lay in the fact that they would—

(1) Secure economy in food and in use of fuel, considerably reduce waste of foods; secure economy in soap, towels, crockery, and other kitchen necessities.

(2) Secure a reasonably adequate supply of food at comparatively low prices; place within the reach of the working classes wholesome food instead of "makeshift" meals; and obviate many of the difficulties of buying, with its attendant waiting and disappointment.

(3) Release many women from the arduousness of domestic life, and perhaps enable some of them to take up war employment.

(4) Free the shops of many customers whose demands are unorganized, thus creating distributing difficulties.

(5) Afford equal opportunities for all classes to obtain nutritious food prepared on modern hygienic principles.

(6) Afford opportunities for reducing the staffs of retailers, refreshment house proprietors, etc., and reduce consumption of paper, etc., used in parcel distributions; and allay discontent in munitions areas.

(7) Individual cooking was waste of labor, health, material, and energy. A thousand homes with a thousand gas and coal fires resulted in a multiplicity of operations essentially wasteful.

In the same interview, Mr. Spencer suggested that cooperative effort between the local authorities and eating house proprietors in large provincial towns might lead to a big system of "national restaurants." (This forecast is interesting in view of the fact that the restaurant movement was still growing when the armistice was signed. See p. 42.) It was expected that in the new ventures which were to combine kitchen and restaurant, 25 per cent of the food cooked would be consumed on the premises and 75 per cent be taken away. It was hoped that the public would come to use the kitchens as they use municipal trams, gas, and electricity.

The first public order concerning national kitchens was issued February 25, 1918. It had become evident that the food regulations resulted in hotels and restaurants reducing the quantity and quality of food given to their customers, but without any reduction in prices; in some instances prices were actually increased.[2] Seeing that this situation was likely to become an actual hardship the ministry of

---

[1] London Times, Feb. 5, p. 9.

[2] National Kitchens and Restaurants in England, by Phillip B. Kennedy, London, July 19, Commerce Reports No. 185, Aug. 8, 1918.

food took the step to assist the public. This first order; "Defense of the realm act, 1918, No. 223," enabled the food controller to establish national kitchens. This was supplemented by local authorities food control order No. 2, 1918, of February 25, and statutory rules and orders of February 26, 1918. Later, the ministry of food issued a booklet explaining to local authorities the procedure to be followed in establishing national kitchens.[1]

Under the new order, the number of kitchens has increased rapidly. In November, 1917, there were in existence 161 central kitchens; in March, 1918, 250, and in July, about 1,000 national kitchens. Only the three or four kitchens opened as experiments were under the direct management of the ministry.

The original agreement between the local authorities and the ministry of food with reference to the financing of the kitchens was, that 25 per cent of the initial capital outlay would be given by the ministry, 25 per cent lent, and 50 per cent was to be raised by the local authority, which was empowered by the local government board to charge to the rates any necessary expenses. But in response to representations for an alteration regarding this grant, the Treasury agreed in June, that instead of a grant of 25 per cent followed by a possible loan of 25 per cent, the imperial exchequer would grant a loan free of interest for the full amount of the approved capital outlay on the establishment of a kitchen, such loan to be repaid by the local authority by 10 annual installments, the amount to be secured by a statutory mortgage which the local authority would be authorized to give.[2]

In May, 1918, it was announced that a districting scheme had been formulated for the establishment of national kitchens, the districts to coincide with the areas of the Food Commissioners. A divisional director was to be held responsible for carrying out the national policy in each district. The kitchen at Poplar was to be taken as a model.[3]

Inasmuch as the Poplar kitchen has been one of the most successful of the British national kitchens, the description of it may prove of value. The Bow swimmings baths, Roman Road, Poplar, were taken for the purpose, and the most interesting of the innovations connected with it was that a restaurant was arranged at which food from the kitchen could be eaten. It will be remembered that the original purpose of the kitchens was to provide food to be eaten in the home. But it had been found necessary to provide for people who had to

---

[1] Handbook of National Kitchens and Restaurants, National Kitchen Division, Ministry of Food, London, 1918.
[2] Municipal Journal, No. 1326, June 28, 1918, p. 637.
[3] London Times, May 29, 1918.

eat at hotels and restaurants, on whom the food regulations had proved to be a particular hardship.

The cooking in the Poplar kitchen is done by steam, for which appliances were already installed, and by electricity. The electric cooking apparatus comprises a treble-oven electric range, a three-compartment baker's oven, a carving table and hot cupboard, several boiling plates, a couple of grills, etc. Four boilers, each with a capacity of 24 gallons, are available for preparing soups, stews, and stock. This kitchen is open 11:30 a. m. to 1.45 p. m. and 5 to 8 p. m. It began in March, 1918, to serve about 1,000 portions daily, but in May the portions had increased to 2,300.

Not only have residents in this part of Poplar welcomed the opportunity of obtaining cheap, well-cooked meals, but the employees of neighboring works, school teachers, and others go to the kitchen for their midday meal, and a large number of children call at the baths for their dinner on their way home. In many cases women bring their dishes soon after the kitchen has opened, and, by getting dinners ready cooked, save fuel, money, and labor.

The daily bill of fare is, generally, as follows:

DINNER 11.30 A. M. TO 1.45 P. M.

Soup	1d. per half pint.
Fish pie	3d.
Meat roll	4d.
Roast beef or mutton, per portion	4d. or 6d.
Greens	1d.
Potatoes	1d.
Milk pudding	1½d.
Fig pudding	1½d.

SUPPER 5 TO 8 P. M.

Fish roll	3d.
Shepherd's pie	4d.
Cold roast beef	4d.
Pickles	½d.
Stewed apples and custard	1½d.
Suet pudding	1½d.[1]

This kitchen reported in May, that after provision had been made for cost of management, for estimated rental value, interest on redemption of capital, renewal of plant and contingent liabilities, a profit could be made with the prices quoted above at the rate of from 40 to 50 per cent per annum. With a system like this, waste can be avoided, a considerable saving effected in fuel and labor, and good nourishing food provided. Expenses are reduced at the Poplar kitchen by the system of service. Tickets for a meal are bought at an office. In exchange for them the food is obtained at a long table and brought with knife and fork and spoon to the tables. Attendants clear the tables of the used plates, cups, and saucers (the cafeteria

---

[1] London Times, Mar. 27, 1918, p. 8.

method). A penny extra is paid for restaurant service. Those who took the food home originally brought their own vessels and were charged the eating-house prices. More recently special containers have been supplied by some of the kitchens, for the use of which the patron makes a small deposit.

The equipment of the national kitchens is constantly improving. Since they were begun, large firms have been working on the standardization of the utensils, until now, any good trade journal has advertisements for the equipment of these kitchens. The standard number of patrons is 1,000. The experience and advice of some of the pioneers in the work is interesting and valuable, to show the problems already solved, as well as those awaiting solution. One of the early successful kitchens was that at Reading, which was able to feed 5,000 children sent from London in the winter of 1917–18 to escape the air raids.

Central kitchens for the provision of meals for necessitous school children had been established in Reading in 1907. Of the two central kitchens in existence, it was decided to use the principal as the first communal kitchen, which was opened September 3, 1917. It is situated in a thickly populated district and is a part of a disused school building.

A large room is divided into a kitchen, 25 by 20 feet, and a boiler room. In a room adjoining 200 children can be fed. There are packing and distributing rooms on the ground floor, and a large store on the upper floor.

The original furnishing of the kitchen consisted of three steam coppers of 80, 60, and 55 gallons capacity, respectively. A gas stove was hired from the local gas company. A large teak sink for washing up, and a white glazed sink for the preparation of vegetables, etc., were provided.

List of utensils.

Description.		Approximate cost (England, 1918).
2 Lovelock mincers, No. 4	each	34s.
1 potato chipper		20s.
1 bread machine		30s.
1 weighing machine (to 4 hundredweight)		£5 10s.
2 pairs table scales		9s. 6d., 12s. 6d.
1 set of measures	per set	5s.
2 wrought iron stock pots with taps		28s., 36s.
2 oval iron boilers	each	8s.
1 oval tin boiler		3s. 6d.
1 fish kettle		6s.
3 1-gallon tin cans	each	2s.
24 baking tins	do	1s. 6d.
4 skips or wash-ups	do	3s. 6d.
3 buckets	do	2s. 3d.
2 enamel colanders	do	2s. 6d.
1 meat saw and cleaver	do	3s.

Description.	Approximate cost (England, 1918).
2 sets of carvers and steel_____	16s.
1 set of French cook's knives_____per set__	10s. 6d.
6 vegetable knives _____each__	6d.
1 flour scoop_____	2s.
1 conical gravy strainer_____	2s.
12 tinned iron and wooden spoons_____each__	6d.
12 stone jars (7-pound jam jars)_____do____	6d.
6 enameled bins_____do____	6s. 6d.
3 mixing basins_____do____	3s.
6 basins_____do____	1s. 3d.
6 pie dishes_____do____	1s. 9d.
6 large meat dishes_____do____	9s.

This equipment was adequate for meals for 1,000 children, but inadequate for a communal kitchen designed to cater to the public. The following apparatus was therefore added:

Description.	Cost.
1 Portway fuel roasting oven with pyrometer_____	£32 18s. 4d.
1 Wright's pudding steamer_____	£31 2s. 6d.
1 Welbank boilerette_____	£1 10s.
250 tinned iron pudding basins_____per dozen__	3s. 6d. to 5s. 6d.
6 dozen basins or moulds_____do____	2s.
200 patty tins, 4½ and 5 inches in diameter_____do____	1s. 3d. to 1s. 6d.

For this extra equipment, the borough council made a loan of £100, to be repaid from the income of the kitchen.

Kitchen staff, wages, and duties.—1. Female superintendent cook. Wages, £2 weekly and food. A woman with wide and long experience in catering, responsible for the cooking and with complete control of the staff. She carves and serves the roast and boiled joints of meat.

2. Assistant cook, £1 weekly and food. Assists cook with puddings, pastries, etc., also with carving.

3. Male assistant, 14s. 6d. weekly and food. Assists cook with minor kitchen duties, weighing of meat, boiler work, cleaning of coppers and ovens, etc.

4. Three women, each 15s. weekly and food. One prepares vegetables and washes cooking vessels. Another packs and sends meals to centers for necessitous children and attends to general duties. The third waits upon the cooks and serves at the counter.

5. Server (part time), 10s. weekly and dinner. Is at the kitchen 3 to 4 hours daily. Assists in serving out portions.

In addition, a female junior clerk from the education office acts as a cashier and sells tickets. No extra payment is made for this work, but an apportionment is shown in the financial returns.

The supervision of the staff and work is entrusted to the meals superintendent of the education committee, who buys all the food.

The hours of the staff are: Women, 8 a. m. to 5 p. m. daily; man, 6.30 a. m. to 5 p. m. daily. The kitchen is open to the public daily, Sunday excepted, from 11.30 a. m. to 2 p. m.

Suitable printed notices of entrance and exit, instructions to the public that they must provide their own basins, plates, etc., are posted in conspicuous places. Copies of the day's bill of fare are exhibited outside the building and near the cash desk. On entering, the customer buys at the cash desk tickets to the value of the food desired. A separate ticket is given for each dish asked for, to aid in the record. The customer receives food at the counter in exchange for the vouchers, and leaves by a separate exit.

The kitchen buys the tickets, priced and printed, in rolls, 6d. for 500, 10½d. per 1,000. Each ticket is numbered. This numbered ticket system provides an easy method of checking the cashier's ticket account and cash. A typed form is filled in by the cashier each day, and has spaces and entries for each kind of ticket. The number of tickets used and the ticket numbers are also recorded, and each return supplies daily an accurate record of the number of portions sold, with the total amount of cash taken.

Spartan economy is employed. Everything is weighed. A small stock board is kept constantly in use. The cost of each dish is very carefully calculated, and an allowance in the selling price is added of 33⅓ per cent to 40 per cent for capital, working, and other charges. A daily cash account is prepared. The expenditures are for wages, administration, rent and rates, insurance, fuel. cleaning, depreciation of plant and utensils, and actual cost of the food used.

This kitchen can provide a good meal for from 6d. to 8d. The cost of the meal is the actual cost of the kitchen, 4d. each for dinners, and 2d. for breakfast. It serves on the average 675 meals a day to all classes. At first the poor were the main purchasers, but the class of customers has steadily improved. An account is kept with the Reading education committee by which the kitchen feeds necessitous school children.[1]

The superintendent of another successful communal kitchen gives the following advice as to installation and equipment of a kitchen:[2]

The first move should be to get together a small committee of practical and willing workers. Suitable premises come next, centrally located in the quarter to be catered for and spacious enough for all culinary requirements. They should have the following minimum accommodations: (1) A lofty, well-lighted and well-ventilated room for cooking and selling; (2) a large storeroom, dry and well ventilated; (3) a spacious larder; (4) one or two dressing rooms for the staff. A good cellar would be a great addition, for the storage of potatoes and other vegetables.

[1] Municipal Journal, Jan. 11, 1918, pp. 36–41.
[2] Local Government Cronicle, No. 2676, Mar. 23, 1918, pp. 216, 217.

Cooking room, storeroom, and larder should be fully equipped before work is started.

If gas is to be used for cooking, ventilation and also provision for the escape of steam must be well looked after. The use of the newest types of boilers and steamers makes this absolutely necessary. Economies might be effected by borrowing or hiring spare pots and pans from private-house proprietors. Cast-iron utensils, if carefully looked after, keep better in use than idleness. Any aluminum ware that is wanted should be bought outright. Enamel cooking pots should not be used in communal kitchens. The committee will have to decide the number, type, and size of the larger utensils, taking into account the number of customers expected. For the purchase of such articles it will be most economical in the long run to resort to the best and nearest firms. The latest types of boilers and steamers save time and labor every minute they are in use and pay for themselves in this way in a short time, while the older kinds are a perpetual source of worry. The staff should include these persons:

Superintendent; a reliable person with experience in cooking—a woman of good position who will have the entire management in her hands, subject to the control of the committee.

An assistant superintendent, cook, and two kitchen maids, chosen with the help and approval of the superintendent.

Volunteer helpers sell the food and help in rush hours; those accustomed to the people, who live among them, and know their tastes and the value of food. One volunteer is responsible for the cash desk. She and her assistants give out tickets of different values for cash payments. The day's menu, with the price per portion, is posted on the entrance gate, with a duplicate on the cash desk. The food-sales women take over the tickets presented to them by the customers and place them on an upright file, which is beside each dish, with the name of the contents of the dish on a card. Before the seller leaves, she counts the number of portions she has sold and leaves it written on the file. The superintendent verifies the file records and posts them in the daybook. The food prepared for sale has already been entered. What remains unsold is counted. The cash desk furnishes her with the money taken in. She compares that with the food sold, and can see at once if there is a discrepancy.

Two volunteer helpers come to the storeroom daily. One issues all stores asked for by the superintendent and keeps the record in a daybook. The second sees to renewing supplies, assists the other, etc. An accurately kept storeroom daybook is a necessity.

One of the cooks assists the superintendent by taking charge of the petty-cash book. She records all daily supplies which come directly into the kitchen—fresh meat, milk, bread, etc.—and takes all correspondence off the hands of the superintendent.

By the aid of the storeroom book, the petty-cash book, the record of the daily takings in cash, a weekly record of gas expenditure, liabilities for rent, rates, etc., a correct weekly account is furnished to the kitchen committee.

The electric tram has been used in England not only to deliver meals, but for cooking in transit. Such a car was fitted up in April, 1918, by the Halifax corporation tramways committee, whose chairman is Alderman Spencer, the director of national kitchens. A single-deck tramcar was fitted with ovens and cookers and served with electricity from overhead wires. At one end of the car is a cash box where orders are taken and tickets issued. The food is served from the sides of the car. It is prepared at the central kitchen and cooked in the car.

The Halifax tramcar kitchen, which is capable of supplying about 800 portions, is equipped with an electric cooking plant; 2 baking or roasting ovens, 32 inches high by 22 inches wide by 21 inches deep, fitted with 6 racks spaced 5 inches apart; size of each rack 18¼ by 19¼ inches. Sheet metal on angle-iron framing is used. The loading is 16 kilowatts, divided into 4 sections, controlled by 4 quick-break rotary switches fitted on the oven framing. These are 24 heating elements, 12 on each side, interchangeable and easily fitted. For steaming, there are 4 steam cooking ovens, each 16 by 16 by 24 inches, with 4 shelves. There is a 25-gallon boiling pan. The ovens will cook 720 portions of pie in 2 batches, 600 fish cakes in 1 batch, 360 milk puddings, or 108 pounds of bread. The 4 steam cooking ovens cook 1,152 dumplings in 2 batches, 160 pounds of potatoes (320 portions), etc. The whole cooking space is 10 by 5 feet 9 inches by 5 feet 6 inches in height.

The firm of manufacturing electrical engineers which made the appliances for the Halifax tramcar kitchen has placed on the market a complete equipment for an electrically-run kitchen. Their advertisements make the claim that electricity gives 10 per cent more weight cooked meat from the same weight of raw meat than any other method of cooking; it calls for no flues; there is no loss of heat; and it is said to be the most hygienic method. The standardized equipment for 1,000 persons manufactured by this firm is made of the following items:

Description.	Operation.	Cooking output (approximately).
3 electric ovens, each 7½ cubic feet capacity.	Roasting and baking..........	100 pounds of meat (per 3 hours); 54 pounds of bread (each oven, per hour); 360 portions of meat pies; 180 portions milk puddings (per hour); 300 fish cakes (per hour).
5 electric steamers, each 5½ cubic feet capacity.	Suet pudding, potatoes, and other vegetables, etc.	Each steamer, 80 pounds potatoes (per ¾ hour); 245 dumplings (per ¾ hour); 250 portions suet roll (per ¾ hour); 125 meat puddings (per ¾ hour).
2 30-gallon boilers, with lifting grids.	For vegetables...............	150 pounds of potatoes or similar vegetables (each boiler).
2 30-gallon soup boilers........	For soups....................	About 60 gallons of soup equals 640 ⅔ pint portions.
1 10-gallon water boiling urn...	For tea making and sundry purposes.	Where supplied with hot water at about 130° F. the capacity is about 320° ½ pint portions per hour.
1 hot cupboard with hot top...	For plates and for keeping cooked food warm.	500 plates in one batch, or 250 plates, and 40 to 50 dinners in dishes with suitable piling up covers.
1 boiler plate, with 3 burners and griller.	For frying, grilling, toasting, making sauces, gravies, and other sundry work.	Griller will do 6 rounds of toast, 5 minutes; 12 small chops or steaks (per ¼ hour); a number of utensils can be kept simmering or boiling on the 3 burners.
3 solid-top hot plates..........	For keeping trays of food, taken from ovens and steamers hot whilst being served.	Simply for use adjoining the serving counter; are very strong and will stand any weight.
1 boiler (burning coal, coke, or refuse, with 70-gallon storage tank).	For supplying hot water to feed the electrical steamers, boilers, urns, etc., and for washing purposes.	Output, 25 gallons boiling water per hour, or will raise 60 gallons of water to 130° F. in 1 hour.

A great deal of careful thought was given to the equipment of the kitchen at Hammersmith, a large one, supplying about 6,000 customers a week, which probably represents 12,000 to 15,000 consumers.

Two factors were deemed of great importance: First, a bill of fare which could be worked to with the least variety of appliances, thus limiting labor and cost while increasing possible output; second, the preparation and sale of foods that could be warmed up most successfully without spoiling * * *. The ovens are gas heated and brick lined; a type which is best for continuous, uniform cooking * * *. The kitchen being large, it was possible to introduce a steam-generating boiler for those cooking processes which can be done by steam, consequently the meat boilers are steam-jacketed, the pudding steamers are heated by a supply from the boiler, while the sink water is also heated by steam. Baking, as indicated, is done by gas-heated ovens which are known as pastry cooks' ovens. The vegetable boilers are gas heated, not steam, and this was due to the less first cost of the gas boiler.[1]

The report just quoted also describes the equipment of the Westminster national kitchen, which is a gas kitchen. It offers a wide choice of cooked foods and has appliances similar to those found in a canteen or middle-class restaurant.

A useful form of steam cooker is made of tinned sheet steel, really a simple sheet-metal cupboard, about 20 by 20 by 24 inches or larger, with perforated shelves. The special detail is the bottom, which is formed of an open water pan holding sufficient water for one steaming. Under this bottom a gas ring is set to boil the water. The door must fit well. An aperture at top, usually one-half inch in diameter, lets the steam escape and prevents undue pressure. The steam escapes into the kitchen or may be led away through a pipe. Nothing could be simpler or less expensive to make, and it is quite safe, because steam under pressure is never required for this work.

Another necessary appliance is the hot closet, which may be made of black sheet-iron plates riveted on angle-iron framing or similarly stiffened. Hot closets are obtainable from the regular manufacturers, but these are usually of cast plates, and the top is sometimes heated independently to serve as a hot table and to provide accommodation for a bain-marie pan and carving dishes. Where, however, low cost is of importance the simple black sheet-iron cupboard is found sufficient. A useful size would be 6 feet wide, 2 feet 6 inches high, 2 feet front to back. If the top is required to be stiff enough to serve as a warm counter or table simple means of staying can be devised. The heating of a hot closet can be readily done by a few No. 2 luminous gas burners. Ten or twelve to a 6-foot closet suffice, for a fairly low temperature is all that is required.

Another form of appliance, sometimes partly sunk into the counter, sometimes independent, is the soup and vegetable warming tins. These need no covers if a quick service is expected. The vessels are of tin, about 20 by 14 inches by 12 inches high, quite plain inside, but arranged with a suitable middle rim or projection outside, so that the lower half, or thereabouts, drops and rests in a pan of hot water.

When we turn to a study of the menus of the British kitchens, it becomes clear that their problems of organization and equipment are

---

[1] The Ironmonger, Mar. 9, 1918; quoted in Commerce Reports, Apr. 15, 1918.

vastly different from those of the kitchens on the continent, most of which keep to a menu of broth, stew, or soup, which simplifies the whole process of preparing, cooking, transporting, serving, and apportioning the food. Little other equipment is needed at such central kitchens than mincing or chopping machines and boilers proportioned in number and size to the public for whom provision is made; and these proportions have long since been carefully worked out and standardized by the Volksküchen. For transportation, large cans or vessels are easily obtainable, and a dipper is about all that is necessary at the distributing center. Where ordinary care is used the food will require no reheating, and there is no problem of loss of weight or nutriment. The same conditions hold true of the Italian kitchens. Mr. J. E. Ham, American consul at Turin, in a report to the State Department on the first communal kitchen in Rome, opened December, 1917, gives the following facts with reference to the meals and equipment: "There are 4 kettles, with a capacity of 250 liters (75 gallons). The meals consist of a soup of vegetables, 30 centimes ($0.06), and 120 grams (4 ounces) of boneless meat, with vegetables, 90 centimes ($0.18)."

The British ministry of food, in the installation of the national kitchens set for itself the problem of interfering as little as possible with the food habits of the population, and of making the transition from home cooking to the buying of food ready cooked as easy as possible. While it had under advisement the education of its public in the use of foods of greater nutritive value and in many cases more available than the more familiar foods, it did not make the mistake of Holland in selling at the kitchens the foods already unpopular through tradition or special circumstance. Instead, the kitchens started by serving foods that were appetizing, popular, familiar, and attractive.

The menus had to be prepared with a view in the beginning to the preparation and sale of only those foods which could be warmed successfully without spoiling. It will be remembered that the original plans for the kitchens called only for the sale of foods to be taken away. The modification of this plan by opening restaurants in connection with the kitchens has changed the planning of the menus, also the hours during which the kitchens are open. The early kitchens were in most cases open from 11 a. m. to about 2 p. m., but at the present time there is great variation in this matter.

In the Hammersmith kitchen a weekly bill of fare is used. A typical menu is: Mutton broth, 1d.; mutton pie, 3d.; cheese cutlet, 2d.; potatoes, 1d.; sirup roll, 1d. Except for occasional rissoles, it may be said that the meat is always in pie form, an arrangement which simplifies the choice of appliances, and facilitates cooking, service, and the convenience of the public, which has to carry away and warm up the food. The meat pies are baked in small tins, so that one whole pie goes to each purchaser.

A typical menu of such kitchens as those of Westminster, Ealing, and Reading, which provide a wider variety, is as follows: Scotch broth, 1½d.; fish roll, 2d.; vegetable pie, 2d.; mince, 4d.; roast meat, 5d.; potatoes, 1d.; parsnips, 1d.; ginger pudding, 2d.; plain pudding and sauce, 2d.; baked rice pudding, 1½d.

The Halifax tramcar kitchen served the following menu on its first day:

```
½ pint soup_____ 1d.
Dumpling_____ 1d.
Vegetable pie_____ 4d.
Potatoes_____ 1d.
Rice pudding_____ 1½d.
Ginger pudding_____ 2d.
```

A kitchen at Buckingham Palace Road, London, offered in January, 1918, the following menu:

```
Vegetable soup _____ 1d.
Beef stew _____ 3d.
Meat pies_____ 2d.
Roast joint _____ 4d. and 6d.
Steamed potatoes _____ 1d.
Cabbage_____ 1d.
Treacle pudding _____ 1½d.
Rice pudding _____ 1d.
Extra portions of gravy _____ ½d.
```

The central cooperative kitchen at Holloway, conducted by the Northern Polytechnic and serving 2,500 patrons daily, offered this menu in February: Soup, beef stew, meat pies, roast joint, tripe and onions, baked herrings, potatoes, cabbage, treacle, or rice pudding.

The Chelsea national kitchen offers an appetizing and varied bill of fare. There is always a whole fish sold at a higher cost than made-up fish. A midday bill of fare comprised barley soup, 1½d.; baked haddock 6d.; and kedgeree, 3d.; the vegetables were potatoes and braised onions. There were three kinds of sweets and savory rice at 3d. Cold meats are on sale in the evening.

These menus give some idea of the kind of food sold, its variety, and the range of prices. They are chosen from menus given at perhaps the darkest period through which England has passed with respect to her food supply, and reflect the care with which the authorities dealt with the food habits of the nation.

The causes of success and failure in the national experiment in communal kitchens made by Great Britain are intimately connected with the question as to their future. The one chief criticism, that they are a step away from family life and in the direction of communism, was met at the time of their inception by the answer of their sheer, dire necessity. That the problem of actual food scarcity, for which they were offered as a partial solution, will continue into the after-the-war period has been generally accepted as a fact.

There is little doubt that the kitchens have successfully met the temptation to profiteering which arises in times of crisis. An editorial writer in the Manchester Guardian, March 12, 1918, said:

London is beginning to realize how enormous is the profit of the caterer in all but the most humble restaurants. The broad fact is that most restaurants have steadily cut down their portions of unrationed as well as of rationed food, and have increased their prices to a point far beyond that of the commodities.

That commercial enterprises could not be trusted to step in to meet the need is shown by the writer in the Quarterly Review for January, 1918, when he makes the nice distinction between a "commercially profitable demand" and a "national advantage," and says:

Until the standard of life in the more populous centers has been raised to a point at which the demand for ready-cooked meals of satisfactory quality becomes effective, the private cookshop is likely to concentrate on a few popular but frequently wasteful and comparatively expensive foods.

A contributing cause of the failure of some of the earlier kitchens was the use of too much volunteer and untrained help. Workers inexperienced in such catering did not understand either the proper combination of foods to secure an adequate and attractive diet or how to purchase and serve to avoid waste of money and materials.

It was evident that this danger was recognized, for the members of the ministry of food repeatedly deprecated the use of volunteer helpers in their public utterances, and expressly stipulated that the kitchens must "pay their way." It is also often observed by those interested that the presence of volunteer workers "creates an atmosphere of condescension and patronage." The founders of the Italian, Austrian, and German kitchens advocated their use, as lessening the gap between the social classes. But this way of lessening class-conflict does not seem to appeal to the Britisher. This is particularly true in kitchens which hope to reach the middle class.

The following reasons were given for the non-success of some of the earlier English kitchens:[1]

(1) The expensive system adopted of a central kitchen with distributing depots instead of having self-contained kitchens.

(2) No proper system of deciding the sale prices of the articles sold.

(3) The fact that voluntary helpers sell food at depots without the assistance of a paid supervisor.

(4) That the tickets used are not properly checked with the number of portions sold.

(5) That the portions returned and portions sold do not agree with the total number of portions sent out.

---

[1] Municipal Journal, June 28, 1918, p. 687.

(6) The monotony in menus—too much fried food, using a quantity of fat for cooking and frying purposes, and an insufficient quantity of vegetables, sauces, and gravies.

(7) Selling of cold food.

(8) That there has been no system of valuing stock each week.

Mr. Cox has strongly recommended that the present system of control kitchens be discontinued, and that in place of it a self-contained kitchen with a restaurant should be established; that a storekeeper and cashier should be appointed, whose duty it would be to issue stores daily to the cook in charge, with a statement of their value. Care should also be taken to see that the profit on the food sold be about 33⅓ per cent of the cost of the raw material, and that in no case should it be less than 25 per cent.

The writer of an open letter written to the Manchester Guardian attributes some of the hindrances to the success of the national kitchens to the ministry; others are deeply ingrained in the habits of the people; others are matters of organization, administration, and experience. Although this writer looks upon the kitchens as primarily a war measure to provide for a reliable distribution of cheap and wholesome meals, he adds:[1]

There may very likely be a permanent place in our social system for the national or municipal kitchen. It may revolutionize the methods of providing family dinners, and ultimately domestic cookery may have to be reckoned among the lost arts, but with a compensating gain to woman from freedom from toil and worry and monotony in the service of the home.

A much copied exchange used in labor papers and entitled "National Kitchens Popular in England," says:[2]

The question naturally arises: Will these institutions, which are proving of such immense economic value at the present time, survive the war? If we admit that the unparalleled position which woman at the present time occupies in the industrial world may have effects beyond the wildest dreams of speculation, it is not difficult to make out a case for the survival of the national kitchen.

It is significant in this connection that the platform of the Woman's Party in England includes the plank:

Food rations, accompanied by the development of communal kitchens, so as to economize domestic labor, reduce food waste, and guarantee to the people the best possible food at the lowest possible prices, cooked in the most skillful way, so that its full nutritive value may be secured.   .

---

[1] Reprinted in Local Government Chronicle, May 25, 1918, p. 341.

[2] The Square Deal. Devoted to the interests of organized labor. Vol. IV, No. 18, Aug. 16, 1918.

Since the above was written the following note has appeared in the Canadian Food Bulletin (No. 21, Ottawa, December, 1918): "A scheme for a national kitchen at Bath, England, has been rejected by the city council. It was stated that Liverpool has closed five such kitchens after losing £1,000 on each."

The immediate future of the British national kitchens seems to lie in the development of canteen and restaurant facilities. The national restaurant in New Bridge Street, London, to be run as both kitchen and restaurant, was opened as a model. The cooking is done by steam, gas, and electricity, the roasting by electricity, and the boiling by gas. It was opened on June 26, 1918, and its immediate success showed the need for these restaurants in populous neighborhoods. Shops, offices, and homes in the vicinity may send and collect their own meals or have them delivered at an extra charge of a penny. Others have since been opened in London, Leeds, Glasgow, Manchester, Newcastle-on-Tyne, Brighton, Cardiff, Birmingham, and Bristol.

The representative of the United States Department of Labor in Great Britain writes of the New Bridge Street restaurant as follows:[1]

The moderate price restaurant keepers * * * have been much opposed to this undertaking of the ministry of food, claiming that it could not succeed without a Government subsidy, owing to the low prices charged and the large portions served. The figures given in the report for four weeks show, according to the director, a profit of 70 per cent per annum, and, as has been said, " suggest that it is really possible to supply nourishing food in satisfying quantities at low prices and yet obtain a very substantial profit." * * * At none of the other eating places are such large portions served as at the National restaurant, and at most of them the prices are slightly higher. If there is any difference in the quality of the food served it is all in favor of the Government restaurant.

One is much impressed at this restaurant by the class of people who use the place. They are all rather prosperous-looking middle-class people, and I fear the people for whom the place was supposedly designed do not get much benefit from it. * * * *

The menu for the day, with prices, hangs outside the door. About a dozen people are admitted at a time, and they, having decided upon their order, ask the cashier just inside for checks for the total amount they are to spend * * *. Then one proceeds to the long serving counter and gets whatever one desires on a tray, somewhat as in our caféterias, except that each dish is served by an attendant who takes the necessary check in return. The tables are set [by waitresses, who also clear them] with all the requisite cutlery and drinking water and glasses. The china and cutlery are most satisfactory. The service is rapid, all things considered. On the whole, however, the manager might learn much in that respect from a study of those marvelous Chicago cafét(e)rias * * *.

I lunched on soup (2d. [4 cents]), rice pudding (3d. [6 cents]), bread and butter—three slices—(2d. [4 cents]), and coffee (2d. [4 cents]) ; total, 11d. [22 cents], and I have not yet ceased being astonished at the quantity and quality of everything * * *. There was almost no noise and no loud talking. Everyone was apparently enjoying his lunch and having a restful break in his day's work, as well. That is more than we can say for ourselves in Washington at lunch time * * *.

---

[1] Cost of Food in National Restaurants in London, by N. C. Adams, Monthly Labor Review, November, 1918, pp. 121-122. See also Municipal Journal, July 12, 1918, p. 729, and article by P. B. Kennedy in Commerce Reports, U. S. Department of State, Aug. 8, 1918, pp. 520-522.

Prices in the first-class restaurants and the moderate-priced places in London are practically the same as in America, but I have never seen a place at home where I could get for the money as satisfactory a lunch as I had at this restaurant.

At about the time of the opening of the first national restaurant the ministry of food announced that it would take over from the former contractor the three canteens in the Southampton dockyards and convert them into national kitchens, reequipping the building with steam and electrical cooking arrangements. There are some 10,000 employees in the yards.

As one reviews the history of the British national kitchen movement, it becomes evident that it has not been clear sailing, in spite of the courage, enthusiasm, and resourcefulness of the responsible members of the ministry of food. The lessons to be learned may be summarized from the pages of the writer in the monthly review before quoted:

Public kitchens, to be successful, must be opened in the right neighborhood.

Kitchens must be located in attractive premises, in prominent positions.

Kitchens will have to offer such value for the money as to compete effectively with the privately cooked meal.

Kitchens will have to study the tastes and prejudices of their patrons, introducing unfamiliar dishes gradually.

Public kitchens will have to make the most of their advantage as public and patriotic institutions, enjoying the support of the food authorities. They will need the advantage of centralized buying at wholesale prices; they will need help in the shape of information, instruction, and advice; and they will need the " good will " attached to their public character.

The history of the cooperative movement in America, up to the great war, is an epitome of attempts at the development of agencies which undertook to relieve the housewife of some of the burdens of the individual kitchens. American individualism, the enormous distances covered by the States, the variety of peoples, customs, traditions, and an underlying conservatism which was a part of the social inheritance from Puritanism, are all but a part of the reason for the slow growth of movements which would bind communities closer together. There have been isolated cases of sucessful coopertive stores; there are successful experiments here and there in cooperative housekeeping; there are to-day small community kitchens which have a degree of success. Miss Fee, supervisor of the kitchens of the Association for Improving the Condition of the Poor of New York City, told the writer that at a dietetics conference held recently, when the subject of community kitchens was introduced, to the intense surprise of every one it was found that there were present fifteen women interested in some venture of the sort, none of whom knew of the work of the others. It may be that grim necessity will act as a reagent on the chaos of the present and create a unity which will be essentially American, not something copied from the British national kitchens, still less from the Teutonic Volksküchen with their "soup kitchen" tradition to alienate the self-respecting working and middle class.

All that a preliminary study of this sort can hope to do is to present such material as is available on agencies which have to do with the preparation of food in bulk for use in the home. There are two forms of commercial ventures which have successfully entered this field of which we shall merely speak in passing. The public bakery has to a very large extent superseded home baking in the larger communities. In Europe, many of these bakeries are cooperative; but in the United States they are commercial ventures, more or less successful from the dietetic point of view. The exigencies of the war caused a deterioration in the output of many of the bakeries because of the difficulty of making bread in quantities with the modified flour. Many war agencies in various cities have ventured into the field previously preempted by the baker. For example, all of the bread for

44

the city canteens maintained by the mayor's committee of women on national defense of New York City is now baked in the city kitchen.

Another cooked-food agency which has made itself a part of city life is the delicatessen shop. In cities where apartment-house life is the home life of the mass of the middle class, where there are many women who work but who prefer to eat at home, the delicatessen shop in its better form has been a boon. It is true, however, that it has not been an unmodified blessing from the standpoint of health or financial economy. While there are no statistics available, there has been enough investigation of the delicatessen trade in some of the large American cities to make it a certainty that much of the food used in certain types of shops is of low grade, bought on the verge of spoiling and salvaged with dressings highly seasoned and decorated. A study made by a worker for the board of health in one city of the sources of supply for delicatessen shops uncovered the fact that very little high-grade material was used. This is probably equally true of other cities. The food is, therefore, relatively expensive. The study alluded to showed that the delicatessen shops are prospering under war conditions because of the demand for women in labor. That there are large night sales is indicated by the difficulty in getting delicatessen shops to conform to any closing program. When the dealers were asked to close early in order to save light, heat, and food, they made the very interesting remonstrance that their best patrons were those employed late at night. It would seem that any city community kitchen venture should take this statement into account in planning its hours for serving the public, if it desires to reach the public to which the delicatessen shops cater. It would also seem that there could never be a better time to bring the delicatessen shop into line with other agencies in the conservation of food and the preservation of the national health. It can be made a more important institution than it now is if the suspicion of the quality of its product can be removed from the reputable dealers by adequate investigation and supervision, with a consequent standardization of products.

No account, however brief, of ventures in the large scale preparation of wholesome food to be consumed in the home would be complete without telling the story of the New England kitchen, an experiment undertaken in the early nineties " to determine the successful conditions of preparing by scientific methods, from the cheaper food materials, nutritious and palatable dishes, which should find a ready demand at paying prices." According to a statement made by Mrs. Ellen H. Richards in the preface to the story of this kitchen written by its founder, Mrs. Mary Hinman Abel, the success of the kitchen was directly due to Mrs. Abel's hard work as well as to her unusual ability, enthusiasm, and ready tact. In other words, the situation then did not directly call for the kitchen, but the kitchen had to educate its public.

The New England kitchen was not founded primarily to pay its way. A fund had been provided; those who took the fund were left free to work according to their discretion. That it was on its feet financially in two years was owing to its proximity to a school to which it served lunches (see p. 18).

The business side of this kitchen venture was never prominent. Mrs. Abel was able to proceed with the venture, according to the terms of the gift, without giving a thought to the cost. The price of the food sold was meant to cover little more than the cost of production. But the kitchen taught the founder many things about the method for a paying kitchen. As to organization, she advises "a stock company with a board of directors, scientific and medical men, with a delivery system for choice foods, food for invalids, bread, etc." One of the great obstacles to the success of such ventures Mrs. Abel believes to be "the mixed nationalities and varied tastes of the inhabitants of our cities." This kitchen later became a part of the plant of the Women's Industrial and Educational Union of Boston, which has been a pioneer in much scientific work connected with the problems created for women by their absorption into industrial life, and whose recent study of "The Food of Working Women in Boston" shows conclusively how serious a problem is created for the Nation by the underfeeding of so large a percentage of the future mothers of the Nation during the most important period of their lives.

Mrs. Abel has kept a record of community ventures in kitchens and cooperative housekeeping over a long period, beginning with the eighties. They are so much alike in their leading features that to tell the story of one or two is to give the substance of all. In one thing they agree—few have been permanently successful.

A kitchen in Carthage, Mo., was in operation from September, 1907, to January, 1911. In this case the patrons came to the house in which the kitchen was located for all their meals. Each family furnished its own table, chairs, dishes, linen, silver, and also such table decorations, jellies, pickles, and other "extras" as it desired, thus following its own tastes and standards. The tables were sufficiently far apart to permit of intimate conversation at each, a feature which was believed to increase the home-like feeling of the place. This feeling was carefully fostered by the paid superintendent, and much of the success of the venture was laid to her ability to make the members feel that their individual tastes were not disregarded. Its failure was attributed to the steady rise in price of materials and labor. Those members who could not afford to pay the increased cost for keeping up the original standard apparently preferred to do their economizing in the privacy of their own homes. Of course the decrease in membership raised the overhead cost per capita and thus forced an increase in the charges out of proportion to the increase in the cost in food and wages.

To provide the original equipment for the kitchen an assessment of $3 per adult and $1.50 per child was made. There were originally sixty members, including 10 or 12 children. This money was used to equip the kitchen, a cheap but large ice box, a cook stove, cooking vessels, serving table, furniture for servants' rooms, and muslin curtains for the entire house being provided.

For the first three months the weekly price was $3 for adult, $1.50 for child. As the number decreased and the prices of food advanced this amount was increased. When the number decreased to 50, the price of board advanced to $3.50. In the fall of 1909 the number decreased to 45. For the next two years board was $4 a week, $2 for children. In 1910 there was a very bad drought through that part of the country and vegetables and fruits were very high. Potatoes sold all the fall for $3 a bushel. The number of members had fallen off still more and an extra assessment of 20 cents per week, per capita, was made for the last twelve weeks that the place remained in operation.

The equipment purchased with the original assessment was in a dilapidated condition at the end of four years. There was nothing of any value but the stove, which was sold at one-half of the price paid for it originally. The curtains and a few things were sold to a second-hand man. The money obtained for these was used to make good the deficit in the final accounts.

Another cooperative venture in Evanston, Ill., which attracted a good deal of attention, lasted four years. According to this plan, food could be sent to the kitchen from the homes, cooked and returned.

Charlotte Talley, writing of "A Cooperative kitchen that is meeting a need in its community," says that it took this kitchen two years to develop in the minds of its founders before becoming a reality.[1] A society was first organized. Although $1,000 was desired as a working capital, the venture started with $900, 90 persons having taken one share each. A communal dining room was tastefully equipped, but meals were also sent to the homes in automobiles hired for the purpose. Maids were sometimes sent from this kitchen to serve the meals in the homes, and catering was done for entertainments. The prices charged for the meals were, for subscribers: Breakfast, $0.25; luncheon, $0.35; dinner, $0.50. Ten cents additional for breakfast and luncheon, and 15 cents more for dinner were charged to nonsubscribers. A fee of 10 cents was charged for de-

---

livery. The food-carrier used was the Swedish container consisting of a tier of enamel or aluminum dishes which fit into a receptacle like an ice-cream container.

This kitchen had five workers: Manager, assistant manager, cook, butler, and waitress. "On a week investigated, 420 persons were served. The per capita cost was $0.31. On this amount the kitchen broke even."

The writer has no data as to the effect war conditions has had on any of these ventures, with the exception of the Montclair community venture, probably the most successful up to the war of any of the American experiments. War conditions made it necessary for it to go out of business, not, however, without having taught many valuable lessons in the plan of capitalization and organization which may be used later by others who believe that the marvelous increase in cooperation in European countries will finally have its counterpart in the United States.

Improvements were gradually made by the education of dealers through these ventures in the kind of food carrier needed. The kitchens found also that they had to be less educational at the start and cater more to individual tastes.

The following story of the brave beginning and untimely end of a communal kitchen in New York in 1918 holds in it much that is suggestive. This venture does not stand alone.

The kitchen whose story is to be told was opened by a volunteer workers' organization in a congested district of upper New York, where all nationalities and religions are present. Many of the children of the neighborhood were known to be suffering from malnutrition, and living conditions were bad. It was the purpose of the women interested to cater to the most needy part of the neighborhood.

The money for equipment was donated, but it was hoped that the kitchen could be made to pay running expenses. On this basis, it was calculated that from 35 to 40 per cent must be added to the actual cost of the food, in order to make the kitchen pay its way. Rental was $35 a month. A good cook was secured for $12 a week. She was given two meals a day. Her helper was paid $1 a day, with meals. The other helpers, four or five in number, were volunteer workers.

The equipment was simple, as it was not intended to provide a wide range of cooked food, but rather to specialize in certain dishes which were well known and liked. Among these were fish cakes, clam chowder, and stews, preferably beef stew with vegetables. Baked apples and prunes were the only desserts prepared. The apples were popularized at three for 5 cents, but it was found necessary to increase the price to four for 10 cents. The fish cakes were standardized at three for 5 cents, although money was sometimes lost, which had to be made up on soups and stews. All the buying was done in the neighborhood by the supervisor, who was one of the volunteer workers. This was thought best for two reasons—in order to win the friendship of the community and in order to buy in small quantities and spare the expense of storeroom and ice. As little as possible was carried over, so that a small ice box was all that was necessary. Large quantities were never prepared. Even with the fish cakes, which were most in demand, it was found that they were much better when prepared in small quantities and constantly made fresh. In answer to the question whether recipes can be "doubled up" with like results, the workers in this kitchen were emphatic in their negatives. They also said that their customers were as quick to note and complain of any change as customers of higher priced caterers would be.

The kitchen opened very successfully, catering to from 130 to 150 women a day. Although it had been intended to reach the more needy women of the neighborhood, the kitchen was embarrassed to find that it was more patronized by the prosperous and thrifty element. After the venture was well started, however, it was found that a prejudice was growing against it, not because it was a charity, but because the spiritual advisers of the patrons thought it was a "communistic venture." Just whether this was the main cause of its decline is not clear. It was said here, as elsewhere, that a change of cooks might influence the patronage over a long period, emphasizing the fact that the reputation of a kitchen, as of any commercial venture, must be maintained unimpaired. The use of so many volunteer helpers is another reason given. Still another was the great fluctuation of prices in the markets and the difficulty in getting some of the most necessary articles.

The supervisor of this kitchen said that a similar one could be equipped for $800 to $1,000, provided the gas company would loan a stove. The most expensive article in the equipment was a 30 gallon copper kettle, an indispensable article.

An effort to meet the needs of American middle class families has recently been inaugurated under the patronage of some prominent men and women. Its announcements state that the service is:

Designed to meet the needs of the great mass of independent homes * * * not organized as a charity, but as a permanent effort at social betterment, on a sound, self-sustaining basis that will yet save the consumer from commercial exploitation.[1]

The service is designed chiefly for:

The business or professional woman living alone, the young family living on a small salary without maid service, the artist in studios, the large family

---

[1] Prospectus of the American Cooked Food Service, 1 Madison Avenue, New York, N. Y.

In which the mother is verging on physical breakdown through the shortage in domestic help, and others ranging from the isolated occupant of the hall bedroom in a rooming house, to families living in private homes and the highest type of apartment houses.

In an estimate for the economies of this service it is said:

Probably for the majority of patrons the cooked meals are delivered at the home for the same price that the retail buyer would pay for the raw food stuffs * * * Individual economies come through lessened maid service, saving in food waste, and the fuel and upkeep of the individual kitchen.

The first station of this service was opened February 1, 1918, and has been in successful operation ever since. Other stations will soon be opened in cities of varying size.

The cooked food is placed at the central station in containers that keep it hot for several hours. Separate containers carry salads, breads, and cold desserts. These containers are delivered by motor service shortly before meal time and called for at regular times thereafter. Dinners range in price from $0.50 to $1, luncheons from $0.35 to $0.75. It has been found necessary to charge for the bread service because of the rise in prices. Better rates are given for larger families where more portions can be delivered in one set of containers, and special arrangements may be made for children's meals, etc.

New stations of the American Cooked Food Service, the name of this agency which aims to extend its service to every part of the country, are financed partly on a cooperative or popular subscription plan, whereby at least 60 per cent of the stock required to equip and start a station (a total of from $15,000 to $25,000) is subscribed in the locality. This stock is in shares of $100 each, and may be purchased outright in amounts of from one to twenty shares, or, by special arrangements, may be paid for in weekly installments, which it may be possible to save through economies resulting from use of the service.

It is stated by the president of the service that the unit of service on which estimates as to equipment, etc., is to be based will be limited to 500, because beyond that number the home-like quality of the food can not be preserved. In case the demand for service exceeds the capacity of the station, stockholders are given the preference. It is believed from the experience already obtained that a center will be financially self-supporting when the full quota of 500 are served.[1]

The success of this unique experiment will be watched with interest by all who hope to see a standardization of the efforts now being made to meet a situation which is new to Americans, so accustomed to plenty, but now called upon to economize not from purely selfish motives, but in order that we may divide with those

---

[1] This account was prepared in December, 1918.

who are in sore need. Those interested in methods of relieving the domestic labor shortage will also be anxious to see how far it alleviates what in many instances is becoming a hopeless condition.

A similar service, but on a much smaller scale, was privately started in 1918 in Burlington, Vt. The containers are made by a local dealer; they are metal boxes with insulating walls and a door in front into which fit the trays for the different foods. The chief criticism reported of this service was that the menus were vegetarian to accord with the ideas of the founder and manager. It has been is successful operation for some months.

The community kitchen of St. Louis, Mo., is a significant enterprise born of war-time needs. The following description is compiled from correspondence and reports in the files of the woman's committee of the Council of National Defense, with which the St. Louis workers were affiliated. This semiphilanthropic venture closely follows the lines of some of the early communal kitchens in England. Although it is still too young to give any basis for prophecy, there is much for other communities to learn from its methods.

In carrying out the work of the United States Food Administration, it became evident to the women's central committee on food conservation in St. Louis that the problems of the city's congested districts were not the usual ones of the associated charities. They were rather new difficulties born of war conditions and directly connected with the present food emergency. An investigation carried on through the winter months of 1917–18 showed that it was impossible to feed a family of six with an adequate healthful diet on a dollar a day, supposedly the maximum allowance for food on a weekly income of $15.

After the survey that showed the acuteness of the food problem among the working classes, the women's central committee put in the field a corps of visiting housekeepers to work with the associated charities. It was found by these workers that " the old problems of ignorance in regard to home management, sorely aggravated in the present crisis, were found to be playing havoc with the health of the community in the poor districts of the city."

As the months of the winter went by, the idea of community kitchens as the only economic way to solve some of the problems made a strong appeal to the workers. The increasing number of women in industry with dependent families and their impossible situation in regard to providing proper food for their families, finally confirmed the need for radical measures of assistance. It was decided to establish a chain of community kitchens under the direction of the women's central committee on food conservation as a war measure. At these kitchens an adequate ration was to be provided at a cost on the cash-and-carry plan for that part of the population at present unable to feed itself either comfortably or healthfully.

In announcing the decision to open community kitchens, the committee called attention, first, to the importance of keeping up standards of health in war times; second, the experience of our allies in the necessity of proper feeding for factory workers; "third, but not last in degree of importance or seriousness, comes the tremendous responsibility of fostering the health of the children of to-day, upon whom will fall the enormous burdens of the reconstruction period." Attention was also called to the saving of fuel and foodstuffs.

It was estimated that a chain of five kitchens would meet the needs of St. Louis with the food situation as it was in the spring of 1918. The location of the kitchens was to be determined by the poverty of the neighborhood, the presence of factories, especially those employing women, by the proximity of a market, and by the density of population.

The kitchens were to be conducted on the following schedule: In the morning from 6.30 to 8.30, cash-and-carry milk, bread, and cereals will be for sale. At noon the cafeteria will serve a complete meal in a single dish, of soup, with a roll, and coffee. Soup wagonettes will be wheeled to the factories in the neighborhood, each wagon equipped to serve 80 pints, and carrying in attached containers the same number of 2-ounce rolls. A pint of soup and a roll are sold for 5 cents. From 4.30 to 8 the cafeteria will be open for the evening meal, consisting of meat, a vegetable, a starch, and a dessert. Patrons who desire to carry their meal home will call for it in three buckets—one for meat and vegetables, one for the starch, and one for the dessert. There will be full and half portions, the entire meal to cost per person, 5 cents for the half-portion meal and 10 cents for the full portion.

Preparatory work was done in the factories by members of the Consumers' League to enlist the interest and cooperation of the managers. It was emphasized that the kitchen was to be a self-supporting, self-respecting enterprise, in no way to be considered in the light of a charity. It was to be an efficient way of handling the food problem on a community plan. It was purposed to make the kitchen a neighborhood center for information in regard to questions of diet, of general hygiene, and of better home management. It was arranged to have cooking demonstrations and talks given by the St. Louis home demonstration agents of the agricultural extension service.

The money for the establishment of these kitchens was earned through a patriotic food show. Of the $5,000 thus acquired, $2,000 was set aside for the experiment. It was agreed to open one kitchen and run it for several months before opening the other four. The business basis agreed upon was as follows:

The daily overhead was estimated by adding the salaries, rent, light, fuel, ice, to the actual cost of raw materials, plus insurance and depreciation. Depreciation was estimated at 1/365 of the initial investment. To this was added another 1/365 of the initial investment representing the portion of the investment indebtedness to be paid back daily. On some days during the first three weeks of the first kitchen, it was possible to meet this complete proportion. A fault in equipment which made it impossible to take care of the number of people necessary to meet the overhead had to be remedied during the first month. It was estimated on the basis of reports of other kitchens, especially those in Great Britain, that an allowance of 30 per cent over the actual cost of materials would cover the overhead and make the kitchen self-supporting.

The first kitchen, whose initial equipment cost about $1,000, was opened at 1729–1731 South Seventh Street, in a quaint building in the heart of a factory district. There are ten large factories employing many women in the immediate neighborhood. Four day nurseries are filled to capacity in this district, giving proof that the mothers are at work in the factories. Social workers state that there was no more needy district in the city during the winter, 1917–18. A market is within the block, also a cannery conducted during the summer by the women's central committee on food conservation. In the auditorium of a library in the block two cooking schools have been conducted by the committee, one in the spring of 1917 and one this year, with an average attendance of 200 foreign-born women, Poles, Lithuanians, Hungarians, and Germans.

The building in which the kitchen was opened lends itself admirably to the work. The caretaker and his wife occupy one of the two second floor apartments. The wife is an unusually intelligent Hungarian who was quick to see that her home should measure up to the standard of cleanliness in the kitchen below. On the opening day she threw open her doors without any suggestion on the part of the committee, to the guests of the kitchen. It is hoped that this apartment can be made a model for a family of small means. The other apartment is to be made into an old clothes clinic. On the third floor a large store is used for storage of fumigated clothes, and for groceries and supplies. The basement offers storage for the canned fruits and vegetables to be preserved during the summer for the use of the kitchens.

Much of the initial equipment was given below cost by those interested and, in some cases, as an outright gift. The china, shelves, lighting fixtures, wash machines, mangles, water heaters, tea-towel dryers, and gas steam heaters were donated. The cooking equipment consists of two ovens and nine stock pots, heavy copper, standing each on an iron tripod. There are four 10-gallon stock pots, four 10-gallon double boilers, and one 25-gallon soup kettle. The cooking is done in the serving room; a large counter shuts off the kitchen end from the cafeteria. The preparation room in the rear is cemented. Here vegetables are cleaned, groceries received, and a large ice-box located. Uniforms, tea-towels, and dishes are washed in the rear rooms. A model back yard poultry unit has been installed in the back yard by the poultry committee of the production division of the women's central committee on food conservation.

A bill board in front of the building announces the menu for the next day. A large painted wooden sign over the entrance reads:

" THIS IS YOUR KITCHEN—WE DO YOUR COOKING FOR YOU."

The woman in charge of the kitchen has had experience in a similar enterprise abroad. A volunteer worker has charge of the cash register. The women of the neighborhood give much volunteer service. They have hemmed all the dish towels; they have helped with the cleaning; they have washed every utensil and dish that has come into the building. "The purpose from the beginning has been to make them feel that it was their kitchen and their attitude bears proof that this has been successfully carried out."

The seating capacity of the cafeteria is 60, with room to increase it. Within an hour 120 persons can be served at the tables. It was found that about 50 per cent of the customers were for the cafeteria and 50 per cent cash-and-carry meals. In addition to the service at the kitchen, wagonettes take out meals to factories near by. One of the factories sends a porter for the wagonette, and a woman in Hoover costume is in attendance. The kitchen has more calls for this kind of service than it can supply at present, but will make provision to meet it as soon as it becomes evident that the demand is to be a steady one. One of the workers says: "The only way to find out whether an idea is going to be popular is to make an actual experiment."

The cash-and-carry bucket meal is served from the counter. Women leave their buckets on their way to work. The capacity for the evening meal is 250; for the noon hour, 480; at breakfast 960 persons can be served with cereal. Since the cooking equipment is in units it is possible to increase the capacity on two weeks' notice.

It was a question as to whether it would pay to keep the kitchen open on Sunday, but it was thought better to try it out, so meals were served the first three Sundays. There was a loss each time. The kitchen was then closed on Sunday. To quote a worker: "Apparently the women employed in factories the week round like to have a thoroughly domestic time on Sunday."

This wholehearted and carefully worked out experiment in communal kitchens will be watched with great interest. It is too early to venture prophecy as to its permanent value, except on the basis of our previous studies. It is still an open question in America as to whether the enthusiasm of the volunteer worker can make up for her lack of training. And inasmuch as even trained dietitians and cooks were found in England to be bettered by a special training for national kitchen work, it may be best to utilize the good will of volunteer workers in the present emergency. It will be well, however, to remember that in the long run it is necessary to use paid workers who are sure to be in their place at fixed hours and who are more amenable to discipline when an experiment is on its way to become an institution.

The problem of the feeding of school children has been considered in several American cities, but in no such definite and organized way throughout the country as has been done in Germany, and in England since the statistics gathered as a result of the Boer War have brought her face to face with the effects of malnutrition on her population. It had proceeded far enough, however, for such cities as Boston and New York to have well-worked-out plans for central kitchens from which a wholesome meal can be sent to thousands of school children every school day. When the problem of communal kitchens confronted the British ministry of food, it was to the local education boards that they most often looked for equipment and direction, and it was to the dietitians trained for the schools that they looked for the workers in the early national kitchens. It is therefore with some relief that we find in our own country that a worker in the Boston central kitchen has worked out under the supervision of the research department of the Women's Educational and Industrial Union a complete scheme for the equipment of a central kitchen. Information is also available concerning the equipment of the central kitchen of the New York School Lunch Committee. These two organizations have most kindly allowed this material to be printed as appendices to this report. (See Appendix A, pp. 65 to 73, and Appendix B, pp. 74 and 75.)

In a recent attempt to study the system by which lunches are supplied to school children in New York City, the first discovery made was that there is only one New York City agency serving lunches to school children, the New York school lunch committee, 105 East Twenty-second Street, New York. This committee has no connection with the board of education, except that several years ago the board appropriated $25,000 to assist in providing schools with the necessary permanent equipment, such as sinks, gas ranges, copper boilers, closets, tables, benches, etc. There is a Brooklyn school lunch committee with activities confined to Brooklyn; but neither of these school lunch committees is in any way connected with the other, or with the board of education, except in the single case of the appropriation specified above.

The New York school lunch committee has been in the field longest and has in operation a large central kitchen. This kitchen was fitted up at a total expense of about $20,000, through the kindness of a woman interested in the project, and through the grant by the board of education of an old building once used as a school annex. From this kitchen as a center 25 schools are supplied. With its equipment, however, Miss Elizabeth M. Fee, the supervisor, estimates that it is working at only about one-third its capacity. On this basis, it should be serving 75 of the 208 schools of Manhattan and the Bronx. The need for this service is obvious. In a statement made by the committee it is shown that the seven to ten thousand children reached by the school lunch service are only 5 per cent of the children in need of the service in Greater New York.

In a pamphlet on "School Lunches" issued by the New York School Lunch Committee, the following paragraph on "What it Costs" appears:[1]

The committee has constantly aimed to make the school lunch service self-supporting to the extent of covering the cost of the food and its preparation. The cost of equipment and supervision, it feels, ought not to be paid for by the pupils but by the city as a legitimate charge against education. While the lunch sales have thus far always covered the cost of the food, they have never covered entirely the cost of preparing it. The financial statement for the year 1916–17 shows that the receipts in addition to paying for the food, paid for 60 per cent of the labor costs. It is likely that by a wise extension and cooperation of the work, the remaining 40 per cent of this item could also be covered.

Excerpts from the paragraph on "What the Children Eat" are significant in a forecast of what would be one of the problems of a community venture in cooking in an American community, with its variety of race and religion:

Racial and religious tastes and prejudices must be carefully considered in determining the menus offered. In Jewish schools only food which complies with the Jewish religion and tradition is offered; in a similar way racial preferences are catered to in Italian schools. In schools attended by both Hebrews and Italians, the situation is still further complicated, and the problem is met by offering in the menu both Italian and Jewish dishes. * * * The committee has found that the improperly fed child at first rebels against the kind of food

---

[1] School lunches: Association for Improving the Condition of the Poor, 105 East Twenty-second Street, New York.

offered in the school lunch, but that he gradually comes to like it and eventually demands the same kind of food at home. By this rather indirect method the food habits of the entire family are gradually improved.

This same society maintains a kitchen on the west side in a district where many of the mothers are at work all day. It was founded by donation and may be called semiphilanthropic in purpose. It corresponds more closely to the Volksküchen than any kitchen we have hitherto described.[1]

Looking back over the history of group or mass feeding and reviewing the various experiments, both successful and unsuccessful, with a view to the situation in the United States to-day, there are certain conclusions to be drawn. First of all, America has been a land of plenty, and the wars, famines, and pestilences which have been prolonged enough in their effects in Europe to bring beyond the experimental stage such institutions as Rumford kitchens, Volksküchen, cucini popolari, etc., have never come to us. The pressure which will lead to our own experimentation will be not alone the necessity growing out of the war, but something else which is a part of the idealism at the root of the whole-hearted enthusiasm which has energized our war-time efforts. The education of the American people to after-war conditions, in which we may still be responsible for the food of peoples who otherwise would starve, will have much to do in preventing a return to our old laissez-faire attitude toward the world outside America.

There are not more than three agencies for the preparation of food for the household outside the home which can be said to have passed the experimental stage in America. Two of them, the bakery and the delicatessen shop, are commercial in character and are managed by their owners with no immediate concern for the public welfare other than that enforced by our laws. The other venture, still much less mature with us than in European countries, is the organization of school feeding. Such development of this phase of our national life as can be found in cities like New York and Boston gives some material on which to proceed in community ventures. But it must be emphasized that school lunches are never expected to " pay their way " in the same sense as that in which a middle-class community kitchen must pay its way to be self-respecting. The items in the cost price of the food of a community kitchen must include every detail of a commercial venture except the profit to the enterpriser, with a lessened bill for advertising and distribution.

In order that such conscientious experimentation in communal feeding as shall be made in the near future may profit by past mis-

---

takes, there are certain items of practical advice to be gathered from other ventures.

Mr. Harris, in his chapters on cooperation in America, says that a review of cooperative ventures among us shows that there has almost never been a true cooperating group back of the undertaking. A true cooperating group will go into such an undertaking with the purpose of seeing it through; not just to stay in until the novelty is worn off or until hard times appear, as they do at some stage in all ventures. It takes courage, persistence, and business management, as in any commercial undertaking, to make a communal kitchen succeed.

There must be the most careful bookkeeping and checking up of costs from the beginning. Mrs. Abel's suggestion of a stock company, seconded by Mr. Harris, and put in practice by the American Cooked Food Service, is excellent, and a step in the direction of the American way of doing things.

While emphasizing the business side of such a venture, it must be remembered that there is a difference between a " commercial success " and a " national advantage." And one of the most patriotic of the purposes of communal kitchens in America will be to take advantage of our recent awakening to the fact that with the plenty about us we are not " well fed " in a dietetic sense; that we all, rich and poor alike, need to be taught to eat the right things in the right combination. The educational part of this venture is as important in the long run as the economic, even though it may not make so strong a popular appeal.

In America, we have not passed the stage of the volunteer worker. Her energy and enthusiasm have been a national asset since our entrance into the war. It seems almost a gratuitous insult to call attention to her shortcomings when she shows none, in America. But the lesson to be learned from European experience is that she must be used sparingly and under strict supervision by trained workers in a venture which expects to establish itself as a permanent part of the life of a community. The trained worker receiving a regular wage is at her post at regular hours. What she may lack in enthusiasm she makes up in scientific training or technical skill. And the experience of all countries seems to indicate that there is likely to be a certain atmosphere of condescension creep in when volunteer workers are used, to which the English and American attitude of mind is very hostile. The advice of the British ministry of food is to use the volunteer worker not at all, except possibly in small communities. It is barely possible that one of the reasons for the emphatic rejection of the communal kitchen in Germany as a permanent institution, is the long history of the Volksküchen as an accepted charity of better-class women. "In no sense a charity" must be the motto of any communal kitchen which is to be a permanent success in America.

It is to be noted from the experience of England and Germany that the training of the dietitian is not sufficient for success in a communal kitchen. There must be special training for such work over and above the general training. Munich, as long ago as November, 1916, was offering a special training for the public kitchens; and within a month after the kitchens order was promulgated by the British ministry of food, such a course was offered in London. It might be well for all departments in American colleges training women in domestic science to introduce into their courses such special training for communal kitchen work as is available, including special experimentation in cooking in large quantities, together with studies of the food habits of our population. It is to be remembered that the dietitian can not ride roughshod over the customs and traditions of the various races and religions, even though she may invoke the authority of science in her support.

And finally, we still have almost everything to learn. We shall therefore make mistakes. Workers must especially remember that in fairness to all, failures must be reported as frankly and fully as successes. But if there is some central organization through which the successes and mistakes can be pooled, we shall learn quickly. We shall start, as in the war, with the advantage of the experience of others on which to build. Pure imitation will not do the work. The initiative peculiarly the faculty of the American soldier is present in the rest of the population, and will be used to adapt agencies for meeting the food situation as well as for inventing other tools for winning the war and for meeting the problems of the after-the-war period.

CONCLUSIONS.

When this survey was undertaken it was thought that such a study might make possible a definite answer to the question whether or not some form or forms of group or community cooking could be recommended for adoption as a general conservation measure in the United States. Whatever might have been the case had the war continued, the situation is now (January, 1919) by no means sufficiently acute to expect success for such a radical change of habits on the part of any large number of families. Nevertheless it may be worth while to state briefly some of the general conclusions to which a study of such enterprises leads.

These conclusions are based not only on the material included in the earlier sections of this report, but also on opinions expressed in conversation with persons who have had practical experience with such work. Many of these workers were unwilling to be quoted officially, but a safe generalization from their personal opinions is that in America there is at present nothing encouraging to the enthusiast on communal cooking. The causes for failure in the past they consider practically the same as those for the failure of most cooperative enterprises in this country—unwillingness of Americans to submit long to the restraints which cooperation requires, and a lack of leaders who combine adequate ability in planning, buying, cooking, and serving food with general administrative ability.

This does not mean that local enterprises undertaken to meet some special needs may not be as successful as a considerable number have been in the past. Indeed, it is possible that these will be more numerous in the next few months and that a few may become permanent institutions for the benefit of special groups who for one reason or another find the preparation of food in the home especially difficult and uneconomical.

If such attempts are made, it is very much to be hoped that they will be reported freely and with as much detail and frankness regarding failures as regarding successes. Many pioneers in this field have been too disheartened to give others the benefit of their experiences. In a line of work so little understood and so full of pitfalls, each worker needs to know what to avoid as well as what to do, and a failure, carefully analyzed and reported, may help as much in the end as a chance success.

The form of organization and financing likely to prove most successful will vary according to the conditions under which the work is done, especially the character of the group which is to be served. Of the three general types—cooperative, charitable, and self-sustaining with limited profits—the third seems most promising because most in accord with American customs and ideals. Apparently we shall not come to cooperation of the Rochdale type in this country until economic pressure is much greater than at present. While we are ready and eager to extend charitable aid in cases of distress, we prefer to consider this as an emergency measure and to try to remove the underlying causes of the distress rather than to continue alleviating it by almsgiving. It seems to us more in accordance with our democratic tradition to develop an institution which pays its way throughout, giving its financial backers a legitimate but carefully limited profit on their investment, and its patrons whatever advantages of price may come from large scale operation, reduction of profits, etc. Even with this type of organization, we can not hope for lasting success unless we provide strict business methods and well-trained workers. Many experienced observers believe it is equally important to rule out such unpaid assistance as free office space and volunteer helpers.

There seems to be a difference of opinion as to the number of patrons necessary to make a group cooking center self-supporting. Estimates run from 100 to 1,000. The American Cooked Food Service limits to 500 the number to be served from one station, because it can not retain the homelike quality of the food when catering to a larger number.

There is similar divergence of opinion as to the best method of purchasing. Some prefer separate purchasing departments, some leave the marketing to the supervisors, some buy only in large quantities, some partly in large, partly in small. Several kitchens patronize local retail markets. All agree that the purchaser must be thoroughly conversant with marketing conditions and be in constant touch with the person responsible for planning menus.

Most experienced workers do not believe in planning menus too long ahead because of the possibility of unexpected developments in the market. All agree that to repeat the same list of menus week after week is bad policy because the patrons notice and dislike the appearance of certain dishes on certain days. A resourceful planner can avoid this without difficulty, and even a less competent one can adopt a schedule for a few more than seven days and so lessen the unpleasant effect on the patrons.

It is not feasible to increase the number of portions to be made according to a given recipe by simply increasing the quantities of the ingredients. Larger quantities may require different methods of manipulation and almost invariably require differences in the proportion of flavorings which can be learned only by testing.

The number of workers required to a given number of patrons has been worked out in several cases. In a standard British public kitchen commencing with 1,000 portions, a staff of six trained persons is required; a supervisor, two cooks, two kitchen maids, and a cashier. It has been found that the average output for each member of the staff is 200 portions until 1,200 are reached, and beyond that number 300 portions for every additional member of the staff. When this statement was submitted to the head of a large central kitchen in this country and to the supervisor of another smaller kitchen which serves about 250 families, they called attention to the fact that the English cooks and general workers are usually more carefully trained and more accustomed to certain specific kinds of work than are American workers. Moreover, there is a carefully worked out special training now given to these workers in European countries, which would need to be provided in America if the kitchens were opened in any great numbers.

The central kitchen of the school lunch committee of the New York Association for Improving the Condition of the Poor employs 90 persons in its service to 35 schools. The plan of the Boston kitchen calls for a kitchen superintendent who is a trained domestic scientist, two cooks, a storeroom woman, and three kitchen women. This is for the central kitchen alone, and does not include the service in the schools. The workers in the American Cooked Food Service state that this question is still in process of standardization with them. The labor situation in the United States makes this matter an especially difficult one at present. The social stigma on domestic service of all kinds, felt more keenly in America than in European countries, and the tempting openings in other industries, make it very difficult to obtain competent help. The system of bonuses adopted in the British kitchens, and the appeal to personal interest in the success of the kitchen might prove stimulating enough to warrant a trial here. In the semi-philanthropic kitchens, in many cases only one worker, the cook, is paid. In others, one regular helper is added. The cashier and those who serve are volunteer workers.

There is comparatively little information as to the exact amounts of food, fuel, and labor saved by group cooking, or of the reductions in cost which it brings. One difficulty in such calculations is of course that so far no method has been worked out for valuing the unpaid labor in the household. An attempt to do this in a cooperative canning kitchen run by the Federal Food Board in New York

City was significant as to the attitude of some women on this point. The workers in this kitchen included women from the neighboring tenement district and the arrangement was that they were to be paid in fruits and vegetables canned at the kitchen. The women refused to consider their time as part of the cost of the product because they resented the idea of having a market value placed on their work. It is true that the labor in the home is not so wearing as the kind of work which these women could get if they went out for employment. They keep their own hours, can rest when they are tired, and do not work under supervision. The report of the New York school lunch committee calls attention to the fact that one cause of malnutrition among children is that in so many cases the mother saves her strength and money for the evening meal when the father comes home and the children are left to forage for themselves at noon. A curate of one of the city churches said that many of these women do practically no work during the day, but depend upon the delicatessen shops on the block for the food for the family. This statement, however, is contradicted by a well known social worker who has done an important work in the investigation of conditions in the delicatessen shops of the city. These facts are stated, not as bearing directly on the subject, but as showing the extreme difficulty of any standardization of the labor of woman in the home, which varies so greatly from family to family. The demand for married women in war industries can hardly be taken as giving a wage norm. But the permanent after-war demand should give us valuable and reliable standards for the economic value of women's work, for which we have always had need in order to answer this question as to the equation between the " value in use " and the " value in exchange " of woman's work.

There are interesting answers to the question how the patrons take to the idea of public kitchens. One kitchen was well on its way to success when the gossip of the neighborhood circulated a report that it was a " communistic " experiment which was aimed at the home. Many of the patrons then stopped coming, as they said, on the advice of their spiritual advisers. This seems a common experience. It can be met by calling attention to the scarcity or cost of food and fuel. and by the necessity of the conservation of the nation's health by the assurance of wholesome food at a reasonable price.

Another kitchen got into trouble in a Jewish community by forgetfulness of the danger of ritual uncleanness. Care must be taken not to offend religious and national prejudices and customs.

There are complaints reported that the food is not so "tasty" as home food. The English kitchens are making a study of flavorings. Then there is complaint of lack of variety and the absence of certain dishes, such as omelets. A common complaint and one to which the final answer is not yet found, is that the food is cold when it reaches the home, whether carried cr delivered, and that the warming-up process takes away from the fine flavor.

The organizers of many group and public kitchens have hoped that the meals might serve as models of proper food selection and preparation and thus lead to better understanding of what makes an adequate and attractive diet. Several have tried printing the nutritive value of the various dishes on the bills of fare, but it seems doubtful whether this has accomplished much. As a rule, the demonstration kitchens, in which instruction has been given in canning, preserving, and the use of food substitutes, have proved a better means of introducing simple instruction in the principles of nutrition. Undoubtedly, there is in this country much more general and intelligent interest in such questions than there ever has been before. This together with the increasing problem of paid labor for women may furnish the incentive to a greater interest in the questions with which this survey deals, and thus lead to practical steps to eliminate, by some means or other, part of the wastefulness and inefficiency which now accompany the preparation of food in many American homes.

Appendix A.

STUDY OF EQUIPMENT FOR A CENTRAL KITCHEN, BY THE WOMEN'S EDUCATIONAL AND INDUSTRIAL UNION OF BOSTON.

INTRODUCTION.

The research department of the Women's Educational and Industrial Union has made a study of the equipment of a central kitchen based chiefly on facts gathered at the kitchen used in preparing noon luncheons for 19 Boston secondary schools. This kitchen inherited the fine traditions of the pioneer effort to apply scientific knowledge to large-scale preparation of food, started under the leadership of Mrs. Ellen F. Richards and Mrs. Mary Hinman Abel, in 1890. The early New England kitchen began supplying hot lunches for school children in 1894, and, when its activities were transferred to the Women's Educational and Industrial Union in 1907, this service was continued. The rapid development of the work made necessary a separate establishment where all foods except bread and cake[1] are prepared. The union has kindly permitted the use of the following extract from a study made by Mrs. M. S. Kirshman, under the direction of Dr. Lucile Eaves.

FORMS OF KITCHEN EQUIPMENT.

Kitchen equipment may be considered conveniently under four headings: First, fixed equipment such as stove, oven, refrigerator, and sinks; second, movable equipment such as tables, desks, etc.; third, the special utensils necessary for the particular types of dishes selected for the menus; and fourth, the general utensils.

The Boston kitchen has six pieces of fixed equipment: (1) Hotel gas range with hood, (2) a double deck oven, (3) a steam cooker with one soup and one vegetable kettle, (4) a refrigerator and stock cooler, (5) a porcelain-lined double sink for cleaning vegetables, (6) a double galvanized-iron sink for washing pots and kettles.

The most expensive and generally needed articles of the fixed equipment are the stove, the refrigerator and the sink. A gas stove is convenient and its use will be economical in many communities. The Boston kitchen uses an eight-burner stove with two ovens below, and has also a separate double-deck oven. When the menu is planned so that the burner and oven space are effectively utilized, a four-burner gas stove is sufficient for serving 500 to 800 persons. The separate double-deck oven is not necessary even in large schools. The gas stoves with heavily insulated walls and fireless cooker attachments are desirable but their initial cost is heavy. If carefully used, however, these stoves

---

[1] The baking for the lunch rooms maintained by the union and for the school lunches is done in a bakery located at the New England kitchen. A brick oven and power mixers are used.

reduce the gas bill over one-half, which is well worth considering. If gas is not available, a kerosene stove probably will answer the purpose even better than a wood or coal stove, as its initial cost is low, and it is economical to operate from the standpoint of both fuel and labor.

Electric stoves and appliances are coming into greater favor. Electricity has nearly all the advantages of gas, is cleaner, requires less labor to run and does not consume the oxygen as does the gas or the coal stove. The even heat lessens the labor of watching the foods, prevents loss from burning, and makes possible uniform standards of production. Power rates must be obtained to make the use of electric cooking and serving appliances economical, but many cities and towns, including even the smaller ones, are willing to give such rates in order to use surplus electric power during the day. Waste in the use of electricity is due to the time which it takes to reach the cooking temperature. This is especially noticeable when boiling water. Some companies are meeting this difficulty by combining the gas and electric stoves so that electricity is used only where long cooking is desired. Fireless cooking principles may be applied and the electricity turned off when the desired temperature is reached. The length of time required to obtain this temperature and the period which it can be maintained without power, should be carefully tested before purchasing any stove which must be used with carefully conserved heat.

The Schenley High School in Pittsburgh, which has its own bakery, has an electric oven, electric dough mixer, and an electric proving box. It also has a gas oven. Recently, a number of commercial cafeterias have placed electric stoves and ovens in their kitchens. High praise is always given by those who use the electric ovens to the standard of the products obtained.

The steam cookers are practical, where it is possible to connect with an outside steam system or where the school lunch department must supply its own hot water. Formerly from 20 to 25 pounds of pressure was considered necessary; it is now known that from 15 to 20 pounds of pressure with longer cooking gives better results. All vegetables are better in texture when cooked by steam; the mineral matter is also conserved. Steam heat is excellent for the making of soups and of white sauce.

REFRIGERATORS.

Refrigerators are for three purposes: First, to cool the materials which are to be served; second, to keep the dishes which are prepared on one day for use on the next; and third, to care for leftovers. The first is important since nearly all foods are served either cold or hot; the second is not necessary unless one kitchen is serving several schools; the third is of minor consideration since with the careful estimation of the requirements, the leftovers should be negligible. A refrigerator should have such insulation as will maintain a temperature between 40 and 50° F. There should be complete circulation of air from the ice chest through the other compartments and back over the ice. There should be perfect drainage and the lining should be seamless so that every part may be cleaned easily. There is economy in the consumption of ice if the refrigerator is small enough so that the ice chest may be kept full all of the time. With the ice compartment in the upper part of the refrigerator, it is possible to drain the water from the side into a container where foods may be cooled easily and quickly before placing them in the ice chest.

An outside door to the ice compartment is sometimes convenient for filling, and ice may be saved during the cold months by opening this door. On the other hand, this arrangement is less important than having the refrigerator near the place where it is needed. In one kitchen visited the refrigerator was over twenty feet from the stove and the work table. The insulation which does not let out the cold should not let in the heat, so that, if necessary, a well-insulated refrigerator may stand near the stove.

An artificial ice plant may be economical if it can be connected with the power which is used for some other purpose. The Schenley High school in Pittsburgh has this system. At the Boston kitchen, ice is used. The refrigerator and stock cooler are built on the west side of the kitchen. When many hot dishes are made on one day to be held over for delivery on the following morning, a large refrigerator is necessary.

SINK.

There are five requisites for a good sink: It should be durable, and of a material easily cleaned; it should drain well; the plumbing should be open; and it should be of such a height that the worker will not need to stoop. Porcelain is the best generally used material. An enamel iron sink may crack. Other materials used are galvanized iron, wrought iron, zinc, slate, soapstone, and a composition such as "Albarene." A commercial sink with open plumbing is far better than a zinc or slate sink set in a wooden frame, as the cracks in the latter make them hard to clean. Soapstone sinks often drain poorly, and the same is true of the galvanized-iron sinks, although they stand harder general wear than porcelain or enamel.

Drain boards can be placed on both sides. If only one drain board is used, it should be at the left. A drain board made of wood with a zinc covering wears well, but the drain boards made as a part of the sink are more easily cleaned. If no drainboard is used, a zinc-covered table at the side will prove satisfactory. Double wash tubs are very useful for the school lunch kitchen: the dishes may be washed in one compartment using a rubber stopper over the drain while the other compartment is used for rinsing. The second compartment may also be used for cleaning vegetables. In the Boston kitchen, it is found necessary to have a second double sink which is used only for the cleaning of vegetables.

Sink attachments of metal plate are good. The faucets should allow a continuous flow of water, as those which must be held while the water flows are consumers of time and energy and do not permit the flushing of drains. High faucets are more convenient. If low, they should be capped with rubber to prevent the breakage of dishes.

The real use of a trap is to make a seal which will not allow foul gases to reach the room. This water seal should be perfect whatever the type chosen.

LABOR-SAVING MACHINERY.

All equipment is selected with the idea of saving labor, but there are certain machines which are known especially as "labor-saving devices." The Boston kitchen has only four machines, aside from the steam cookers, which can be classed strictly as labor saving. They are (1) a meat slicer,[1] (2) a meat chopper and motor, (3) an egg beater and motor with 2 containers of 32 quarts each, and (4) a potato masher. No data are available showing the amount of labor which can be saved by these means. A year ago one school visited put into the kitchen and serving room $1,000 worth of labor-saving machinery which included a steam cooker, a dishwasher and a steam table. The superintendent of the lunch room claimed that the number served had doubled while at the same time two less workers were employed. Time and labor will be saved by installing first the labor-saving machines which are used frequently.

---

[1] The bread slicer is listed under "packing-room equipment." Slicers may be bought which will serve for both bread and meat.

Those used less may be added if the funds and space allow. No new device should be purchased unless it is first thoroughly tested, as the keeping of such utensils in order sometimes requires labor out of proportion to the tasks which they perform.

Movable equipment in the Boston kitchen.

Description.	Price.
1 truck (3 shelves)	$27.50
2 tables, zinc covered, 2 feet 2 inches by 1 foot 3 inches, height 19 inches	12.00
4 tables, zinc covered, 3 feet by 2 feet, height 29 inches	[1]14.40
1 table, zinc covered, 3 feet 6 inches by 2 feet, height 29 inches	[1]4.90
1 table, zinc covered, 3 feet 6 inches by 2 feet, height 29 inches	[2]7.50
1 table, zinc covered, 6 feet by 2 feet 6 inches, height 30 inches (Shelf below)	8.20
2 tables, zinc covered, 5 feet 4 inches by 2 feet 9 inches and 7 feet by 2 feet 8 inches (with elevated shelves and on horses)	[1]11.66
1 desk	[1]7.80
15 wooden chairs with backs	15.00
1 4-foot stepladder	1.20
1 stool, low, for cook to stand on	2.50
1 rack for time cards	5.00
1 platform scales	14.50
1 storeroom scales	[1]4.50
1 clock	2.70
1 electric fan	12.50
12 14-inch japanned trays for employees' lunches	2.70
6 garbage barrels and covers	21.00
2 coal hods	1.30
4 Dish-towel racks	2.40
3 paper towel racks	3.00
2 brooms	.90
2 dustbrushes	1.50
2 dustpans	.50
1 patent mop wringer	2.00
2 mop heads and handles	.70
6 scrub brushes	1.20
4 scrub pails	1.00
6 floor cloths	.38
1 fire extinguisher	6.50
1 fire blanket	1.19
3 pails filled with sand	.75

WORK TABLES AND TRUCKS.

Work tables are either fixed or movable. Fixed tables have several disadvantages; they are more expensive than is necessary for a school lunch kitchen and are generally fitted with drawers which are hard to clean. If a fixed table is used, vitrified tiling makes a good but expensive top; composition tops are likely to crack. But a work table does not have to be expensive in order to stand hard wear; well scrubbed, thick, hard-wood table tops are common in the best equipped hotel kitchens. Oilcloth covering is not durable, and soon becomes unsanitary. Movable tables have a distinct advantage because they can be placed where needed and the floor around them can be cleaned easily.

---

[1] Articles bought previous to July, 1914, cost estimated.
[2] Used to hold the potato masher and motor.

Steel tables, which are often found in hospitals, are excellent if rubber mats are used to prevent breakage. Extra table tops which are put onto horses and fastened to the wall so that they can be let down are useful. There is an advantage in locating tables near the wall becuse utensils and supplies can be kept conveniently on shelves fastened to the wall. If this is not possible, shelves may be built across the top of the table, placing them at the center or back of the table, or making them so that they will slide from one side to the other. A pastry table fitted with zinc-lined flour bins is also good.

Two of the tables listed in the Boston equipment are only 19 inches high— just high enough to hold the utensils into which the soup is strained. When the kettles are too high, the cook stands upon a stool. The low tables are also of the right height to hold the heavy mixing pans. Such tables should have castors, as it was noticeable that the tables with castors stood firmly even under the heavy work of mixing. If the stove and work tables are of the same height, it is possible when the tables are on castors to slide the heaviest utensils from the stove to the tables and to move them wherever desired, thus saving much lifting.

The truck of galvanized iron with removable shelves, also of galvanized iron, is used to carry hot dishes, or to hold them while cooling, before placing them in the refrigerators; also to take food to the packing room. The top shelf of the truck should be of the same height as the stove and tables. Four-wheeled trucks which are easily turned are excellent for carrying food and utensils.

HEIGHT OF EQUIPMENT.

Since stooping and reaching take extra energy, tables, sinks, and stoves should be sufficiently high so that the worker can stand erect, or else a convenient height for sitting at the table. Shelves should not be too high or too low, but adapted to the average worker. The average work table on the market is about 28 inches high; while for the average worker, it should be at least 32 inches. The same question should be considered in connection with the height of the stove and of the working base of the sink which is nearly always set too low.

Special equipment in the Boston kitchen.

Description.	Price.
2 40-quart gray enamel dish pans for mixing	$6.00
3 17-quart gray enamel dish pans for mixing	6.00
4 tin bowls for whipping	5.00
2 15-inch iron frying pans	1.50
8 6-quart agate saucepans and covers for vegetables	2.70
6 18-quart enamel double boilers for white sauce	80.00
2 50-quart copper stock pots for soup	28.00
2 racks for copper stock pots	3.00
6 40-quart cast aluminum stock pots for soup	79.20
12 12-quart block tin milk cans for soup (covers harnessed on)	[1] 15.00
8 10-quart block tin milk cans for soup (covers harnessed on)	[1] 9.60
12 6-quart block tin milk cans for soup (covers harnessed on)	[1] 8.00
8 3-quart block tin milk cans for soup (covers harnessed on)	[1] 4.40
14 6-gallon galvanized iron cans for soaking beans	36.40
1 15-foot hose for carrying water to beans	1.50
1 heavy iron baker's peel for taking beans from oven	1.00
36 8-quart stone bean pots	10.50
48 12-quart round heavy block tin pans for hot specials	[1] 14.00
36 10-quart round heavy block tin pans for hot specials	[1] 9.60
24 8-quart round heavy block tin pans for hot specials	[1] 6.00

Description.	Price.
18 6-quart round heavy block tin pans for hot specials	[1] $4.13
18 4-quart round heavy block tin pans for hot specials	[1] 3.75
12 2-quart round heavy block tin pans for hot specials	[1] 1.10
12 iron baking pans for holding custards in the oven	12.00
24 block tin counter pans for holding custard cups while cooling	6.00
48 dozen white enamel custard cups	52.80
12 aluminum pudding pans for jellies	[1] 7.80
12 12-quart agate pudding pans for jellies	[1] 3.00
6 10-quart agate pudding pans for jellies	[1] 2.52
6 2-quart agate pudding pans for jellies	[1] 1.50
6 1-quart agate pudding pans for jellies	[1] 1.15
2 6-quart enamel pails with covers	2.80
2 strainers to fit 40-quart aluminum stock pots	1.20
2 round block tin hotel colanders (1 fine mesh for rice, 1 coarse mesh for macaroni)	9.00
6 16-quart fiber pails for storage of salt, sugar, etc	1.50
12 1-quart "Lightning" jars for storage	.90
12 1-pint "Lightning" jars for storage	.73

With the above equipment the following kinds and amounts of foods are prepared daily, one variety of each kind being served each day.

Kinds.	Amount.	Full capacity.
	Quarts.	Quarts.
Soup	120	300
Hot special	107	250
Jelly	60	100
Pudding	25	75
Sauce	15	75
Salad	25	50
Custard	[2] 125	[2] 250

[1] Articles also sent to schools; three sets of these articles are kept—one is in use, one en route, and one at the schools.

[2] Individual cups.

MATERIALS FOR UTENSILS IN SPECIAL EQUIPMENT.

Four facts should be considered in the choosing of general utensils: First, the chemical reaction of the foodstuffs upon the material; second, weight; third, durability; fourth, ease of cleaning. The fact that foods vary in the amount of acid or alkali present means that different materials may be selected for different purposes. While the initial cost of enamel ware or tin plate is less, they are not so durable as aluminum. Durability, in the long run, affects the price; while ease of cleaning affects the cost of labor. The weight of utensils is important since the energy utilized varies directly with the weight. Aluminum probably answers all four of the above tests best. The physiological effect of slight amounts of aluminum which may be absorbed with food is still a disputed question, but probably there is no greater danger to health from it than from the enamel chippings which invariably come with the most careful use of the best enamel ware. Cast aluminum certainly is generally considered best for the larger utensils. It is noted that enamel dish pans are used in place of mixing bowls, as they are found better in the large sizes used. When not in use these pans may be hung on nails on the walls. In replacing the round pans made of block tin, used for hot specials, and of agateware used for the pudding pans, it is the intention to substitute aluminum.

General utensils used in the Boston kitchen.

Description.	Price.
3 hand strainers	$1.20
1 flour sifter	.20
2 20-inch handles cast-iron tinned Skimmers	.60
4 1-gallon tin measures	3.00
2 1-quart tin measures	.40
6 1-cup tin measures	.30
1 1-peck wooden measure	.33
6 6-quart enamel pitchers	5.40
3 3-quart enamel pitchers	2.25
1 nickel teakettle	2.00
4 meat boards, 18 by 12 inches	2.00
1 chopping tray	1.10
2 wooden potato mashers (hotel size)	.80
3 wooden butter paddles for putting hot dishes into pans	.60
1 hand potato ricer	.23
1 rolling pin	.20
3 tin scoops	1.20
1 glass lemon squeezer	.03
2 egg heaters	.46
3 heavy-wire French whips	1.65
3 medium-wire French whips	2.70
6 1-quart long-handled dippers for soup	1.20
8 carving knives	8.00
3 chopping knives	1.05
12 vegetable knives	.90
2 18-inch handle iron forks for lifting meats	.80
6 long-handled iron spoons	.30
6 short-handled iron spoons	.30
12 tin tablespoons	.25
24 tin teaspoons	.25
1 ice pick	.20
1 gas lighter	.25

The Boston kitchen is not necessarily a standard for other kitchens in the materials selected. It is, however, a fine example of a reasonably inexpensive outfit capable of turning out a large amount of well-cooked food. The total expenditure for partitions, plumbing, lighting, and all other equipment was only $3,000; over one-third of which was used for the first three items.

NUMBER AND DUTIES OF THE KITCHEN EMPLOYEES IN THE BOSTON KITCHEN.

Kitchen superintendent.—The kitchen superintendent, who is in direct charge of the kitchen, is a trained domestic scientist. The day's orders for dishes are sent to her by one of the clerks; she returns to the clerk a requisition for the food materials required. The superintendent then posts the recipes in the exact amounts required where they are available to the kitchen force. She is responsible for all of the recipes used and is constantly experimenting with them to increase the nutritive value of the food, decrease its cost, and to improve its flavor and appearance. Her desk is so located that she can supervise every part of the kitchen, and she gives such assistance with all parts of the work as is necessary to insure every detail being carried on efficiently. The kitchen superintendent also has charge of the entire building and is responsible for the kitchen and packing-room employees as well as for the janitor.

Head cook.—The head cook begins at 7 in the morning[1] to place the food cooked the day before where it can be quickly sent to the packing room. Her one duty during the day is the preparation of the hot specials.

Assistant cook.—The assistant cook arrives at 6 in the morning in order to prepare the employees' breakfasts. During spare moments of the early morning hours she may assist in frosting the cakes. The assistant cook is responsible for custards, sandwich mixture, and the employees' breakfasts and lunches.

Storeroom woman.—The storeroom woman arrives at 5 in the morning in order to take materials from the storeroom, and make the soups which are prepared just before they are sent out. She attends to the frosting of the cakes, work which is also done in the morning the goods are sent. Every Tuesday and Wednesday she has full charge of cooking the beans.

Kitchen women.—There are three kitchen women who are employed in slicing meats, peeling vegetables, looking over beans, and washing dishes. One of these women arrives at 5 in the morning and cuts all of the bread used in the packing room; another comes at 6 and works one-half of her time each day in the packing room.

Equipment for packing room.

1. General equipment.
A. Stationary:

1 cabinet for left-over breads, galvanized iron, 4 feet 4 inches by 2 feet 3 inches, height 5 feet 20 inches_____ $130. 00

1 cabinet for storing packing supplies_____ 20. 00

B. Labor saving machinery:

1 bread cutting machine and motor_____ 62. 00

C. Movable equipment:

3 tables, zinc covered elevated shelves (shelf for paper below) 4 feet 8 inches by 5 feet, for making sandwiches and packing cakes and sandwiches_____ 65. 00

1 table, zinc covered (on horses, elevated shelves) 7 by 2 feet for packing hot specials, salads and custards_____ 11. 67

1 table, zinc covered, 8 by 2 feet for bread cutting machine_____ 9. 00

1 table, zinc covered, 5 feet 6 inches by 3 feet for bread cutting___ 5. 25

1 table, zinc covered, 3 feet 6 inches by 2 feet 6 inches for bread cutting _____ 4. 90

1 table, 3 by 2 feet for general use_____ 2. 00

1 rack, wooden for cake_____ 23. 00

1 rack for labels_____ 5. 00

1 desk _____ 9. 60

1 desk chair_____ 1. 50

9 chairs used for employees' meals_____ 14. 50

1 clock _____ 2. 70

1 paper towel holder_____

1 paper towel basket_____

1 wastebasket, metal_____ 1. 50

2 brooms _____ . 90

1 dustpan and floor brush_____ . 75

1 dustpan and brush for table_____ . 75

2 brushes for scrubbing_____ . 40

[1] Massachusetts laws allow women to work 54 hours a week. These women work 48 hours, though the hours each day vary from 9 on the first 4 days of the week to 5 on Friday and 7 on Saturday.

C. Movable equipment—Continued.

3 pails, fiber	$0.75
4 floor cloths	.25
2 pails with sand for fire	.50
1 fire extinguisher	6.50
8 food charts for windows	8.00
4 frames for food charts	47.00

2. Special equipment.

A. Packing equipment for transportation:

1 food carrier for use on motor truck	18.50
6 6-bushel wooden baskets with covers and partitions	36.00
3 5-bushel wooden baskets with covers and partitions	15.00
24 2-bushel wooden market baskets, bail handles	18.00
12 2-bushel wooden baskets without handles	27.00
24 custard boxes, galvanized iron, 16 by 16 by $3\frac{1}{2}$ inches	30.00
24 custard boxes, galvanized iron, 16 by 7 by $3\frac{1}{2}$ inches	20.00
24 custard boxes, galvanized iron, 9 by 6 by 3 inches	20.00
6 refrigerator pans for holding ice cream tubs	3.30
2 $\frac{1}{2}$-size barrels, galvanized iron, for waste paper	5.20
4 twine holders for each end of packing tables	1.00

B. Packing supplies (six months' supply):

1,000 paper bags, No. 8 "Torpedo" for groceries	5.10
1,000 1-quart paper food boxes, "Purity," for jams, catsup and mayonnaise	13.50
2,000 1-pint paper food boxes "Purity" for jams, catsups, and mayonnaise	17.50
2,000 1-quart paper pails, "Waxline" for salads and whip cream	10.00
2,000 1-pint paper pails, "Waxline" for salads and whip cream	8.00
10,000 9-inch paper pie plates for pies and cakes	13.00
24 reams paraffin paper	8.40
48 bundles wrapping paper	204.95
1,000 paper tags	.79
8,000 paper bags at schools for individual service of cake and candy	6.91
2,000 paper bags for selling returned food	5.76

3. Utensils:

8 cake knives	7.20
36 tin forks	.88
4 iron long-handled spoons	.20
6 iron short-handled spoons	.30
24 teaspoons	.25

The packing room superintendent has charge of the packing of the baskets which are sent to each school. She checks the orders from each school with the food which goes out; later, these sheets are again checked with the sheets showing the food received at each school. Much of the time of the packing room superintendent is spent in visiting schools under the direction of the assistant director.

Nine women, in addition to superintendent, work from 5 to 8.45 in the morning in the packing room and then go to the schools. These women work 48 hours each week. Other assistance is given by the janitor and also by the kitchen woman who comes at 6 and cuts the bread. Another of the kitchen helpers spends one-half of the day in the packing room assisting the janitor in the cleaning.

Appendix B.

SCHEDULES OF EQUIPMENT USED BY THE NEW YORK SCHOOL LUNCH COMMITTEE, ASSOCIATION FOR IMPROVING THE CONDITION OF THE POOR.

The following lists were prepared by Miss Elizabeth M. Fee, supervisor:

MOVABLE EQUIPMENT FOR A KITCHEN FEEDING 500.

AGATEWARE.

4 pudding or cake pans to fit ovens.
2 ladles for soup or stew (20-inch handles).
2 ladles for cocoa or sauces.
2 double boilers (largest size).
1 8-quart boiler.
8 5-quart pans.
1 10-quart sauce kettle.
2 5-quart saucepans.

CUTLERY.

1 carving knife.
1 butcher knife.
4 case knives.
2 paring knives.
2 long-handled forks (20 inches).
2 small forks.
3 tablespoons.
6 long-handled iron spoons (18 inches).
1 can opener.

EARTHENWARE.

2 4-quart jars (for salad dressing).
25 custard cups.

TIN AND WIRE WARE.

1 apple corer.
6 cup cake pans.
1 colander.
2 dish pans.
1 flat wire whip (whip).
1 round wire whip (beater).
1 dustpan.

TIN AND WIRE WARE—continued.

1 grater for lemons.
12 layer cake pans.
8 loaf cake pans (bread tins).
1 long-handled ladle (20 inches).
1 long-handled skimmer.
1 fine wire strainer (quart size).
1 flour sifter.
1 20-quart soup kettle.

WOODENWARE.

1 bread cutter.
1 broom.
1 whisk broom.
1 mopstick.
1 scrub brush.
1 vegetable brush.
1 washboard.
1 wooden spoon.
2 pulp pails.
1 rolling-pin.
Platform scales.
Small scales.
Hatchet.
1 fry kettle and basket.

TABLEWARE FOR 500.

Glasses.
Sauce and vegetable dishes.
Plates (medium).
Small plates.
Bowls.
Coffee cups.
Trays.

TABLEWARE FOR 500—continued.

Salts.
Peppers.
Butter bowl.
Pitchers for milk.
Vinegar bottle.
Mustard bottle.
Table silver.

MISCELLANEOUS.

1 scrub cloth.
1 dozen dish towels. .
6 oven cloths.
3 dishcloths (for washing dishes).
6 tablecloths.
1 20-quart soup kettle.
1 quart measuring cup.

MISCELLANEOUS—continued

2 ½-pint measuring cups.
1 soap shaker.
1 soap dish.
2 wire dish drainers.
1 glass lemon squeezer.
1 meat grinder.
1 garbage can and cover.
4 crisco cans.
8 gallon cans and covers for beans, etc.
4 1-quart containers.
4 4-quart containers.
6 galvanized covers for barrels; 2 18 inches diameter, 4 20 inches diameter.
4 bread baskets.
2 40-quart milk cans.

EQUIPMENT OF A VOCATIONAL SCHOOL FEEDING 500.

MOVABLE EQUIPMENT.

500 trays.
500 tablespoons.
500 teaspoons.
500 knives.
500 forks.
500 saucers, 5½ inches diameter.
500 soup bowls.
500 bread and butter plates, 6½ inches diameter.
500 meat plates.
3 canisters, small.
7 ladles.
1 skimmer.
2 colanders, large and small.
3 wooden spoons.
1 Chinese strainer, 7 inches diameter.
2 meat forks.
6 cooking spoons.
1 broom.
1 dustpan.
1 washboard.
1 rolling pin.
4 wire egg beaters.
3 agate pudding pans, 10 inches diameter.
3 agate roasting pans, 12 inches diameter.
1 agate pot, 2 gallons.
1 agate pot, 1 gallon.
2 frying pans, 13 inches diameter.
2 frying pans, 9½ inches diameter.
2 white enamel dishpans, 15 inches diameter.

MOVABLE EQUIPMENT—continued.

1 white enamel pot, 2 gallons.
1 agate pot, 5 gallons.
1 agate stock boiler, 8 gallons.
1 wooden army pail.
1 meat chopper.
1 scale, small.
2 steel stock pots.
1 French frying pan, large.
2 garbage cans.
1 grater.
2 bread pans, 6½ by 8½ inches.
1 potato masher, wire.
1 potato pounder, large.
1 mixing bowl.
2 paring knives, 6½ inches.
4½ dozen salt and pepper shakers (glasses, cups, salt, and peppers).
1 bread-cutting machine.

PERMANENT EQUIPMENT.

Meat block.
Scale, Fairbanks' standard.
Ice chest.
Urns, milk.
Urns, coffee.
Urns, chocolate.
Urns, hot water.
Steam table.
Dish-washing machine.
Copper stock pot, 40 gallons.
Steel sink.
Garland range, 2 sections.

SCHEDULE OF STANDARDIZED COOKING APPLIANCES, TAKEN FROM HANDBOOK OF NATIONAL KITCHENS AND RESTAURANTS, ISSUED BY THE NATIONAL KITCHENS DIVISION, [BRITISH] MINISTRY OF FOOD, JULY, 1918.

Description of cooking appliance recommended.	Duty performed.	Number of appliances required for cooking—	
		1,000 portions.	2,500 portions.
(a) 30-gallon water-jacketed boiler, double cased, with rustless cast-iron pan, draw-off taps, lid and strainer.	Various stews, soups, milk puddings, etc.	2	3
(b) 30-gallon boiler, single cased (not water jacketed but otherwise as above), with two wire baskets.	Vegetables (boiled)..........	1	2
(c) Independent cast-iron steamer on stand (simple type), with paper-tight door and having automatic feed; inside size about 7 cubic feet. (c. 1) Steamer to fit into boiling pan, with four wire trays and front door (tinned plate), or (c. 2) Cupboard steamer, independent type, with four wire trays and front door (tinned plate).	Fish, puddings, and vegetables (steamed).	2	3
(d) Vertical oven, fitted with five grids, capable of being adjusted to various heights, about 50 by 24 inches inside.	Roasting and baking........	1 or 2	2 or 3
(e) Boiling plate 4 feet 6 inches by 2 feet 6 inches by 2 feet 9 inches high, on stand, having 6 burners and 1 griller, with single oven under; inside capacity of oven about 7 cubic feet. Alternative to above: Small single oven with boiling plate at one end, resting on feet at one end, and bracketed to oven at other end, above 5 feet 0 inches over all.	Frying, stock, sauces, gravies, etc.	1	1
(f) Serving table and hot closet, size 4 feet 6 inches by 2 feet 6 inches by 2 feet 9 inches high, with plain top.	Keeping food hot...........	1	1

SMALL EQUIPMENT.

2 roller towel supports.
3 menu frames and letters.
1 clock.
3 signs marking divisions of counter for "Meat," "Pudding," and "Soup and vegetables."
3 door mats.
25 dozen basins (enameled), 3 inches diameter.
4 dozen pudding basins (1-quart size).
3 lard tins, 18 inches to 20 inches.
2 dozen pie dishes, 16 inches.
1 milk pail with dipper (4 gallons).

36 baking dishes of various sizes, 28, 20, 18, and 16 inches square, and 2 to 3 inches deep.
Iron saucepans, tin lined, with two handles—
    3 of 3 gallons.
    4 of 2 gallons.
    1 of 1½ gallons.
2 frying pans, 16 inches diameter.
Deep frying pot and tray, 20 inches long.
3 colanders, tin lined, one 18 inches diameter, two 16 inches diameter.

Enameled basins, six 20 inches diameter, four 18 inches diameter.
2 kettles.
2 mincers.
12 cook's knives, 12, 9, and 5 inches.
4 forks.
2 pairs of carvers.
1 steel.
1 chopper.
1 saw.
1 honing knife.
1 ice pick for breaking salt.
6 iron spoons, 12 inches.
6 enameled spoons.
12 wooden spoons, 10 to 24 inches.
2 basting spoons.
3 vegetable peelers.
1 coarse mesh (conical).
1 fine mesh (round).
1 spice box.
1 flour dredger.
1 salt box.
1 pepper box.
6 pot stands.
2 fish slicers.
2 graters.
6 ladles (two of 1 pint, two of ¾ pint, two of ½ pint).
Enameled jugs (two of 1 gallon, two of ½ gallon).
Enameled trays for storing and serving food (12, 22 by 16 inches; 12, 18 by 13 inches).
Scales to 14 pounds.
Small scales to 1 pound.
Pint measure.
A potato washer.
1 corkscrew.
8 to 12 galvanized iron bins for cereals (raised a few inches from the ground on wooden struts or battens).
Wooden bins for vegetables.

2 trestle tables.
Jars and boxes for dry foods.
3 wire meat covers, 24, 20, and 12 inch.
1 chopping block.
Weighing machine (4 hundredweight).
Scales, 56 pounds.
6 scoops.
A raised platform for sacks.
1 bass broom.
1 dustpan and brush.
1 hair broom.
1 vegetable brush.
4 scrubbing brushes.
2 sink brushes.
2 saucepan brushes.
2 nail brushes.
1 set of blacklead brushes.
1 dozen dusters.
1 dozen rubbers.
1 dozen towels.
6 roller towels.
6 hand towels.
2 buckets.
1 mop.
4 galvanized baths, 24 inch and 30 inch.
1 funnel.
1 pair of scissors.
1 tin opener.
2 skimming ladles.
2 wire sieves, 16 by 14 inch (one of finer mesh).
2 vegetable presses.
2 rolling pins, 24 inch.
6 chopping boards, 18 inch and 16 inch.
2 sanitary dustbins (vegetable matter must be kept apart from ashes).
2 soap dishes.
1 dozen dish cloths.
1 pair of steps.
Chef's caps and coats, and serving aprons for staff.

O